COMPETITIVE KARTING

A COMPREHENSIVE GUIDE TO KARTING

by Gary Martin

Library of Congress Catalog Card No. 90-83189

COPYRIGHT 1980,1988,1998 by Martin Motorsports. No part of this work may be reproduced without written permission of the author.

MARTIN MOTORSPORTS

P.O.Box 12654   Ft. Wayne, Ind. 46864

INTRODUCTION

Karting is the most inexpensive form of motor racing. The speed and quickness of the little karts offer the same sensation of speed and competition as does full scale racing action. You just can not buy a kart and be a instant winner. It takes a lot of preparation. It takes a lot of luck to make up for a lack of proper preparation.

Making the transition from running around the backyard in a fun kart to a specialized competition kart is a monumental task. The rookie karter will find it difficult to obtain the much needed information to get started on the right foot. It's for this reason I decided to write this book.

This book covers all aspects of the sport of karting. For more detailed information on 4-cycle engines see our book "4-Cycle Kart Engines". Most of the information presented in this book applies to karting no matter which engine you choose for you kart.

My intention is not to single out any one product as being better than another. My main goal is to inform you of what is available so you can make an intelligent choice of what is best for you. This book will give you more information than most of the current karters had when they first started. I've attempted to cover all the areas of karting so as to provide the rookie with some basic fundamentals in all aspects of the sport. The information presented here has been compiled from my own personal experience, and from talking with several of my fellow karters. I have personally used the products and procedures presented unless stated otherwise. I've tried to make this book as accurate as possible, but rules are constantly changing and prices, ideas, and concepts are forever being revised. For that reason I haven't included specific rules. These are available from the national clubs or other publications which I have listed under Additional Reference Material. I've endeavored to write this book in a non-technical, non-scientific language with many illustrations. It is not my intent to make everyone a national champion but I an hoping to make the beginner a steady and consistent finisher. My only hope is that this book will help the average karter finish more races, be more competitive, and have some fun doing it. See you trackside.

TABLE OF CONTENTS

Introduction to Karting — 1

Purchasing A Kart — 9

2-Cycle Theory of Operation — 13

4-Cycle Theory of Operation — 23

Drive System Preparation — 29

Induction System Preparation — 37

Exhaust System Preparation — 41

Preparing The Braking System — 45

Kart Preparation — 51

Engine Preparation — 57

Accessories — 61

Trackside — 67

The Competition Begins — 75

Related Information — 81

Yamaha — 87

US 820 — 91

Trouble Analysis — 93

Personal Performance Record — 106

Additional Reference Material — 107

A SPECIAL THANK YOU

I wish to thank all the people who took time to answer my questions. A special thank you to all the companies that supplied the necessary information required to complete this book.

THE WINNER

Life's battles don't always go,
To the stronger or faster man;
But sooner or later the man who wins,
Is the man who thinks he can.

Author Unknown

INTRODUCTION TO KARTING

In the last several years karting has evolved from a simple homemade kart running around a shopping center parking lot, to a very sophisticated and complex sport. The little West Bend engines, which just about anybody could repair, have been replaced by a multitude of more powerful and more intricate engines. The shopping center tracks, now non-existent because of rising insurance cost, have been replaced by specially designed tracks on private property. Lawn and Fun karts are still available. However, romping around the backyard can't replace the thrills of competition which are only obtainable on a real race track.

Karting is now more popular than ever, National memberships are up and there are more nonsanctioned tracks than ever before. The caliber of racing and racing machines has continued to grow throughout the years. Karting is still one of the most inexpensive ways to enjoy the thrills and excitement of racing.

Karting is one sport that can truly be enjoyed by young or old alike. Even the ladies are allowed to participate as evidenced by multiple champions, Kathy Hartman and Denise Johnston.

Karting offers something for everyone, Sanctioned karting begins at the age of 5 in the rapidly growing Baby Kart class. Age is no handicap in karting. You will also find several middle aged men driving karts. These older drivers are normally referred to as the local boys, or weekend karters, and they make up the nucleus of the karting community. Most of these men have no illusions of becoming a national champion, because of the time and money involved. They spend most of their karting career at the local tracks, racing just because they enjoy it.

Many big name race drivers have started their racing careers in karts. Lake Speed and Ricky Rudd in NASCAR, Michael Andretti, Al Unser Jr, and Scott Prutt in Indy cars, and almost all the Formula One drivers started in karting.

Normally a person's first association with karting comes in the form of a fun or lawn kart.

The principle difference between a lawn kart and a competition kart is that the lawn kart has a much higher ground clearance. Most competition karts have a clearance of two inches or less. This would hardly be suitable for running around the back yard.

Lawn karts are a lot of fun, but soon the urge to go faster and compete against other drivers starts to grow. You begin to wonder what it would be like to be in a real race. Hitting the apex's, drifting around that sweeping left hander and racing your competitor to the checker flag. The joy and sense of pride that comes with winning a race in front of the family is indescribable.

LAWN KARTS

In recent years the number of lawn kart manufacturers has dwindled to a small handful. Lawn karts are still available from most local kart shops and larger department stores. Most stores dealing in karts will have some lawn karts on display for customer inspection.

Lawn karts are equipped with treaded tires so they can obtain adequate adhesion to the irregular surfaces of grass, driveways, and the like. Generally lawn karts are supplied with 6-inch or larger wheels to gain more ground clearance.

Lawn karts are generally equipped with a 4-cycle engine. The 4-cycle engine is less temperamental and can take more abuse than a 2-cycle engine. The 4-cycle engine runs at a much slower engine speed (RPM) and is not subjected to the same vibrational stresses as a 2-cycle engine. All engines used today are of the horizontal output shaft type, as used on the larger lawn mowers and garden tractors. The engines are normally started with a recoil starter. A 4-cycle engine is much the same as a lawn mower engine and requires no special skills to maintain. Following the recommendations in the owners manual should give you countless hours of trouble free running.

Lawn karts are generally available with a rear axle that is commonly called a "dead axle". The term "dead axle" means that the axle itself does not rotate. The engine only drives one rear wheel. The drive gear is attached to the drive wheel only. Dead axle karts tend to turn away from the drive wheel easier than toward it. Karts are also available with a live rear axle. With a live axle kart the engine drives both rear wheels, however they are locked and when you negotiate a turn one of the tires must scuff. Most local stock cars run a locked rear end. The advantage is that power is applied to both rear wheels when exiting a turn. A live axle kart is less likely to get stuck or hung up in rough terrain.

Most lawn karts are subjected to less than ideal running conditions, so special care should be given to them, The first important step is to clean the air cleaner regularly. Change the engine oil according to the manufacturers recommendations.

You should keep the drive wheel and its bearing as clean as possible. Remove the wheels and grease the axle and bearings a couple of times a year, more often if the kart is subjected to extensive or abnormal use. You should check the play in the drive chain and oil the chain before and after every use. A subsequent section on Drive System Preparation applies whether you have a lawn kart or a competition kart.

Many future karters elect to build their own karts. I must warn you that this is a very difficult undertaking. You will need the services of a welder, and unless you have experience welding yourself or have a good friend who does, the cost of having it done should not be over looked. Plans are readily available on how to construct a kart and will not be presented in this book. The biggest expenses in building your own kart are the engine, wheels, and brake components. You should locate these items before you venture forward with the project.

Lawn karts are available with a bench seat so as to accommodate two people. You should remember that the more weight the kart must carry, the larger the engine needed to achieve satisfactory performance.

One thing some karters like to do is put large all-terrain tires on the rear. This is not recommended. Remember, it's a go kart not a dune buggy. Adding ten or twelve inch tires will reduce the power and torque, thus reducing the karts performance. You'll most likely become unhappy with the performance of the kart and start blaming the engine when the real problem is the oversize tires.

Lawn karts come in many shapes and sizes. Single seat and daul seat. A single seat with a 3hp engine is great for a 5 year old, but for an adult or older childern a 5hp engine is better

Lawn karts can be a lot of fun. It's the type of kart that the very young can use to learn and improve their driving skills. A word or two on safety. Karts are not allowed on city streets. It's very difficult for a motorist to see a kart because they are so low and small. A helmet should be worn at all times. Remember, safety first, it's your head.

Competition karts differ greatly from fun karts. Note the sleek low lines, slick tires, disc brakes, and side mounted engine.

COMPETITION KARTS

The first thing you will have to decide before you purchase a racing kart, is what type of karting you will be participating in. The most popular racing in your area will be determined by the local tracks and drivers. There's basically two types of competition karts; sprint, and enduro. These two types have several classes within each group. The sprint class has a speedway division, as well as special races for dirt and street racing.

The sprint karts are the most common. They are a situp type kart and are generally raced on local short tracks of 1/2 mile or less. An enduro kart differs in that the driver is in a reclining position and has large fuel tanks saddled on both sides of the kart. Enduros are raced on larger road racing type tracks an require more travel.

SPRINT KARTS

Sprint karts are divided into classes determined by engine size and modifications. These classes usually consist of: stock, modified, and open classes. The class structures can vary from track to track depending upon the availability of karts. For years karting was dominated by 2-cycle engines such as McCulloch, Yamaha and several foreign engines. In recent years 4-cycle engines such as the Briggs & Stratton and Honda have become very popular. Due in most part to their simplicity and availability.

The box stock 4-cycle classes are probably the most inexpensive classes to participate in, they are generally powered by 5hp Briggs & Stratton engines. The 4-cycle engine requires less work to maintain than a 2-cycle and does not require an external starter. With a 4-cycle, you simply pull the rope and away you go.

Sprint races consist of three, ten lap heat races or two ten lap heat races and a feature, similar to stock car racing. The format differs from track to track depending on local preference.

A very aerodynamically styled sprint kart. This type of body work is very well suited to high speed paved ovals or street races.

SPEEDWAY RACING

One type of sprint racing which is gaining in popularity is speedway racing. The karts are basically the same as sprint karts, but the races are held on oval tracks normally used for stock car racing. Most speedway racing is on oval dirt tracks, but some races are held on paved ovals. In recent year most manufactures have begun to produce LTO (Left Turn Only) karts for this market. These karts have the frame and the driver offset to the left for oval racing.

DIRT RACING

Dirt track racing is undoubtedly the most thrilling of all the sprint classes. It is also the hardest on equipment. Special care must be taken during preparation of a dirt kart to protect the kart and driver from dirt, dust, and mud. Racing gloves and a scarf are an absolute must. The gravel thrown up from the track is similar to a thousand bees attacking you at once. It will actually sandblast the paint from exposed areas of the kart. The other extreme is the mud after they hose down the track to reduce the dust. It just gets everywhere. It's usually a good idea to let a couple of your competitors go out and run in the track before making your appearance. It this case first is not always best.

Air cleaners for the carburetors are a necessity and most karters go so far as to put a large deflector shield in front of the air cleaner. Some serious karters cover as much of the braking system as possible with a screen to prevent mud, rocks, and pebbles, from becoming lodged in the system.

Treaded tires are the accepted standard, but some karters still prefer to run slicks. A dirt track can become very smooth in the later stages of a race which may help the slicks. There's also the possibility that you may be forced out of the groove on a corner. On a dirt track there's always a lot of loose dirt on the outside of the turns. The combination of loose dirt and slicks will put you into the fence.

Dirt racing can be challenging. Being first on the track can get you a mud bath and a stop at the car wash on the way home.

If the track runs long races some sort of chain oiler will be necessary to keep the chain lubricated.

On short tracks of 1/10 mile or less it's not unusual to find karts that are geared very high. The gearing may be limited only by the size of the rear tires. The chain must not run on the ground. On larger tracks you'll find the karts are geared for high speed and its not unusual to find drums with 16 or more teeth, and bottom gears of 52 or 53 teeth. This is especially true on paved ovals. The engine becomes very important on the larger tracks because you spend most of your time at top engine speeds. Consequently you must have an engine that is well balanced. Low wind resistance and a low center of gravity also become much more important than in the regular sprint classes.

There is considerable difference between running a 4-cycle and a 2-cycle engine on dirt. Because of the nature of the 4-cycle engine, especially a stock one, you must keep the RPM's up and drive the track as smooth as possible. Getting the kart sideways only scuffs off speed. The 2-cycle engines have much more power and a more favorable torque band. The kart can be driven into the turns hard, the chassis set sideways and powered out with the rear riding on the outer edges of the track. This type of racing is similar to full size sprint cars and open wheel modified. You must have lots of horsepower, and even then it's not for the faint of heart.

Dirt tracks tend to be a bit more primitive than asphalt tracks but don't let that fool you. There are some very fast karters running the local dirt tracks. Although it's not the fastest way around there is nothing like powering around a corner sideway. It's a blast.

STREET RACING

Another interesting form of sprint karting is the street races. These races are actually run on city streets, or an appropriate parking lot. Most all street races have at least one long straightaway, so speeds are relatively high. Most tracks have a chicane in the front straight. The chicane's purpose is to slow down the karts and form them into a single line for the scorers. The chicane is quite often the most accident prone portion of the track and some degree of caution is required. The races are normally a timed event of 15, or 30 minutes, so most races tend to be more of an endurance race. The best way to place well is to get a good start, be alert and avoid any crucial driving situations.

No special equipment is needed to participate in street events, any sprint kart is acceptable. You will need to gear the kart pretty low for the long straightaway. A chain oiler helps if the race is a long one.

Street racing does present a few unusual obstacles; the most notable of which are curbs, straw bales, light poles, and old tires. If the course has a rise such as when traveling from one city block to another, the kart will likely become airborne. If this happens, position the kart as straight as possible before the rise so the kart will come down square and in the right direction. If you don't land square the kart will be severely flexed and the chain may be thrown off. When airborne you should deaccelerate slightly so as not to over rev the engine. As soon as you touch down again you can accelerate.

You should always keep your eyes open for dogs and people running across the track. For some reason people love to run from side to side. You should avoid any loose straw which may accumulate on the track. Loose straw is very slick and will undoubtedly cause you to spin out.

The street races are a refreshing change from running the same track every week. They're also good for the kart because they help alleviate any misalignment of the frame which may have occurred from running the same track continuously.

ENDURO KARTS

The name enduro comes from the fact that the race is an endurance race, and normally scheduled for 45 minutes or an hour in length.

An enduro kart differs in that the driver is in a reclining position and has large fuel tanks saddled on both sides of the kart. Due to the lower silhouette of the enduro kart they are capable of obtaining a much higher racing speed than the sprint karts. Enduro karts run on road racing courses such as: Indianapolis Raceway Park, Daytona, Mid-Ohio, Riverside, and Watkins Glen.

Enduro racing is not for a rookie. Both of the sanctioning bodies recommend previous experience in sprint racing before issuing an enduro license. An applicant is first issued a novice license. Then he must attend a special drivers meeting and practice session where he is observed by his fellow karters. After successful completion of his novice race he is issued a provisional license which allows him to compete with other qualified drivers.

SANCTIONING ASSOCIATIONS

There are two major sanctioning bodies for karting in the U.S. The World Karting Association (WKA), and the International Kart Federation (IKF). The sanctioning clubs have set up various classes based on age, weight, engine sizes, and engine modifications, in an attempt to make the sport a fair and competitive one. The classes have been structured so you can start out in the rookie classes and work you way up to winning a national championship. There are advantages to joining at least one of the clubs. In addition to a competition license, you will receive a membership card, jacket patch, decal, competition rule book, technical manual, and a one years subscription to their respective magazine. *WORLD KARTING* is the official publication of WKA, and *KARTER NEWS* is the official publication of IKF.

The monthly magazines are used mainly for race results and updates to the tech manuals. The magazines are available without joining the respective organizations. The WKA and IKF have produced a common technical manual/competition rule book, and included it in their respective magazine. Single issue copies are available by writing the respective organization. The competition rule book contains all the driver and kart requirements for the different classes.

The sanctioning bodies have divided the country into divisions and assigned governors (IKF), and directors (WKA), to cover every state to keep in touch with their membership. The club's magazines contain a list of these governors/directors, their addresses, and phone numbers. These officials are people from the karting community and are glad to help whenever they can. They can tell you when and where some of the local events are taking place.

The club's current addresses are.

World Karting Association
5725-D Highway 29N
Harrisburg, NC 28075

International Kart Federation
4650 Arrow HWY, Suite B-4
Montclair, CA 91763

An enduro kart prvides a very low silhouette for minimum wind resistance. Consequently it's not uncommon for enduros to reach speeds in excess of 130 MPH.

Before you decide which club to join, check into the racing scheduled in your area. Both clubs cover the entire United States, but in any one locality there may be some disparity between the number of events. You don't want to be a WKA member if there are ten IKF races and only two WKA races in your area, or vice versa.

It is not necessary to join the WKA or the IKF to compete in karting. Most tracks run a regular schedule of nonsanctioned races, however many of them do schedule one or two sanctioned races a year, and in order to participate in these events you do need a competition license issued by the appropriate body. Some tracks form their own local clubs and run a number of point races during the season. It isn't always necessary to be a club member to participate in these point races, it depends on the track. Most tracks will allow you to participate at a slight increase in entry fee, however these fees may be quite large at some tracks if they are trying to discourage outsiders. Membership in the local clubs will make you eligible for year end awards and newsletters if they have one. Most nonsanctioned races are run to either WKA or IKF rules although the rules are not always strictly enforced. It depends on the track management or local sponsoring club to determine the rules for nonsanctioned events.

A few of the larger kart shops are listed below.

Russell Karting Specialties
   PO Box 1220
   Raymore, MO 64083

American Performance Products
   11092 Southland Rd.
   Cincinnati, Ohio 45240

American Power Sports
   12300 Kinsman Rd.
      Newbury, Ohio 44065

Sox & Sons Small Engines
   2223 Platt Springs Rd.
   West Columbia, S.C. 29169

KARTING INFORMATION

Obtaining information on karting is one of the most difficult jobs for the new karter. This book should help alleviate that problem, but no one book can tell you everything. The most available source of information is from your fellow karters, However it may take awhile to learn which questions to ask.

A trip to the public library can be helpful if you are mainly interested in lawn karts, but you will find little on competition karts. A list of related books appears in the appendix of this book.

The first place to visit is the local kart track if there is one in your area. A visit to your local kart shop can also be informative. Most shop owners race themselves and have karts and parts on display. Unfortunately, some kart shops can be difficult to locate as generally they are operated in combination with a motorcycle shop. One place to look is in the yellow pages of your phone book under Karts, Go Karts or Motorcycles. You can also ask any drivers you may know where they obtain their parts. It's not uncommon for someone to operate a shop out of his garage. These owners do little, if any, advertising.

Another source of information is catalogs published by the larger karting supply houses. These catalogs contain a great deal of information about available parts, services and current prices. This information can be very helpful to the beginning karter. At the current time most manufactures are offering FREE Catalogs.

Due to the high cost of publication the kart shops do not always print a new catalog every year. If you want the latest catalog available you should call the shop and inquire as to when their new catalog will be available. New catalogs are usually available in the spring. There are several other large shops which do not print catalogs, however they do advertise in the karting magazines.

When ordering parts or supplies from a catalog supply house you will receive faster service if you phone in your order and charge the merchandise to a credit card. The next best way is send a money order. If you are in need of your parts in a hurry do

The baby karts are the newest class in karting. This is something the sport can really use. A true starting place for the youngsters.

The class features a short 32" wheelbase kart powered by a Comer 50cc engine. The class is for 5 to 8 year olds and everybody gets a trophy.

Street racing presents many unique obstacles. The most common being straw and crubs. It's amasing how that straw can just suck you into it. It's a real thrill to speed down a two block long straightaway with people crowding both sides. Especially when one of them decides to run across in front of you.

not send a personal check, unless you are a regular customer most supply houses will not ship parts until your check has cleared the bank. Most shops will ship C.O.D., but you must pay the C.O.D. charges and you must also be home when the shipment arrives. U.P.S. prefers cash, but they will accept checks if necessary. U.P.S. cannot ship to a Post Office box.

Another continuing source of information is a couple of current publications. A magazine called National Kart News and a karting newspaper called The Inside Track. They have race results, tech articles, and lots of dealer ads. You can sometimes get a trial copy if you write and request one. These publications are available from the following addresses.

> The Inside Track
> P.O. Box 601
> 1800 West D St.
> Vinton, IA 52349

> National Kart News
> 51535 Bittersweet Rd.
> Granger, IN 46530

PURCHASING A KART

Once you've been bitten by the karting bug you will need to purchase a kart. The day of spending $200.00 and having a competitive kart doesn't exist anymore. Karting has become an expensive and sophisticated sport. A typical single engine kart cost in the neighborhood of $1500.00 new. A new engine (blue printed costs over $500.00. As you can see, the cost of being competitive is very high. The plight of the low budget karter is much the same as the independent in Grand National racing. The cost of being competitive keeps escalating while the racing budget remains relatively the same.

When you're first starting out there's a lot more to buy than just a kart; you will also need an engine, clutch, exhaust pipe, starter, and a multitude of other small, but expensive items. It's fully recommended that a beginner take the time to shop around and learn what's available. Prices can vary considerably depending on the equipment. Listed below are a few things you should look for.

FRAMES

The question that needs answered is whether to buy a brand new outfit or try to locate a good used one. There are several different makes of frames on the market today, and you should have some idea of what you're buying. The kart shops are willing to sell you any brand name you want, it's up to you to decide what will be the best for you. Visit you local kart shop or shops and see what they have to offer. At this point in your career the brand of kart is probably not as important as its condition.

New or used, the best way to get a good deal is to tour the local tracks and see what's winning, and what most of the other karters are driving. Ask around, most of the guys will give you an honest answer about their kart if you ask. With a little luck you may be able to talk someone into letting you take a trial run.

If you're in the market for a used kart, try and find someone that is getting out of the sport. You can usually get a kart with lots of extra goodies at a reasonable price. This will enable you to pick up an assortment of miscellaneous parts and hardware which would normally cost you several hundred dollars. Try to locate an outfit that is only a year or two old, and then replace the major items one at a time as you become more familiar with the sport. Everybody likes to start out with everything brand new, but the truth is that few karters can afford it, and even fewer have any understanding of what they really need until they gain some practical experience.

You will find karting is like most any other big time racing. There are always a few guys that have the money to buy new equipment every year or two. You can usually get a pretty good kart if you can pick up one of these. These guys usually take good care of their equipment and it should last for several years.

Another advantage of visiting a track is that, as a rule the best buys are never advertised in the paper, but are sold right at the track. At almost every race you can find at least one kart with a For Sale sign on it. Buying a kart this way gives you the chance to take the kart out on the track and try it out. You may not know a lot about karts, but at least you will be able to see that the engine runs, the steering and the brakes work, and the frame or axle isn't bent. A couple of trips around the track will give you a pretty good idea of the condition of the kart. If the kart seriously understeers or oversteers, the frame could be sprung. Another sign is if the kart hops around the corners. Caution must be exercised here because with some tires being used today, Burris in particular, you need to warm them up before you can get a good feel for the kart.

A bent rear axle can usually be detected going down the straightaway at a moderate speed. You will experience an up and down motion of the kart.

One of the most important things to watch for is a proper fitting seat. Is it comfortable? Can it be adjusted? Most of the newer karts have both adjustable seats and foot pedals. Be sure you get a good comfortable fit before you buy. Seats are not cheap but they are available.

You can generally tell how good a kart has been cared for simply by giving it a good visual inspection. You should look closely at the welds to insure that there are no breaks or cracks. Do not buy a kart with drum type brakes if your going to be racing competitively. They are not adequate for todays high power engines. Hydraulic disc brakes are a must.

It's recommended you buy a kart already equipped with wide rear tires. A minimum of 11x6.00-5. If you get a kart with narrow tires they can be converted, but the cost is quite high, and it's not just the cost of the tires. The conversion also requires new rims, or at the least, a wheel spacer and bolt kit. It some cases a longer axle may be required. Few of the older karts have axles wide enough for the increased width of the wider tires. The wide tires help make the kart handle better and almost every one is now running them.

Inspect the wheels for broken or cracked rims and hubs. The tires should have some reasonable amount of rubber on them with no cord showing. Buying all new rubber can be expensive. In excess of $100.00.

ENGINES

One thing to keep in mind when shopping is that the engine is the most valuable part of the system. If you don't have the horsepower you're not going to be competitive. If you don't have the money for both a new engine and a new kart, buy the new engine. A good engine can still be competitive on an older kart, but a new kart with a tired engine just won't make the grade.

There are several different makes and models of engines on the market. Komet, BM, Corsair, Yamaha, and Atlas to name a few. The McCulloch was the most widely used engine for several years but there are few of them left. The Yamaha engine has become the most popular engine in the 2-cycle classes. The Yamaha is a 100cc engine and is generally raced in a class of its own.

In the 4-cycle classes the 5hp Briggs & Stratton is the dominate engine, however: Tecumseh is trying to break into karting with its 5 and 10 HP engines and Honda is very popular in Canada.

Most other engines compete in the limited or open classes. The open classes allow unlimited engine modifications, and some of these engines are very fast, but in most cases speed is gained at a sacrifice in reliability. A new karter should stick with the stock engine classes until he becomes more familiar with karting in general, and engines in particular.

NEW ENGINES

Purchasing a new engine is a major investment. There is more to it than just buying an engine. Have you ever wondered why some new engines seem to run faster than others? Every engine is different. Some may never run as fast as others. I'm sure you've heard of such things as line boring, blue printing, and super stock. I'll try to explain what they can mean to you.

If you are going to do any serious racing with IKF or WKA you will most definitely need every ounce of power you can obtain from your engine, If you are just going to run local tracks you may not need to have the engine line bored, but you'll probably be happier with your engine if you have it blue printed. If you're going to spend the money for a new engine you should go ahead and spend the extra money for a good blue print job.

Blue printing is the machining of the cylinder ports, head and piston fit, to the blue prints of the manufacturer. However in karting it would be more correct to say that the engine is blue printed to the Technical manual. Blue printing is legal in both the IKF and WKA. Blue printing does improve the performance of an engine, however it's not cheap.

Line boring is truing the bore so that it is exactly 90 degrees to the crankshaft, straight and round over the entire length of the bore. You will normally have to take the engine to a reasonably well equipped shop to obtain an accurate line bore. Line boring may or may not be done as a part of blue printing. Be sure to ask so you know what you're paying for. Line boring allows the piston, connecting rod, and crankshaft to operate to closer tolerance, with less friction, so that the engine can attain a higher RPM, and thus produce more power.

Super stocking is another term for blue printing. What ever you call it, you should have it done anytime you purchase a new engine. This is true whether the engine is a 2-cycle or a 4-cycle.

The engine should be broken in before having it blue printed. Idealy a couple of weekends of racing is best.

USED ENGINES

Buying a used engine is pretty much a guessing game. If you're buying it with the kart and can take it out on the track and run it, then you'll have a better idea as to its true condition. The most important thing to know is, probably, the cylinder bore size. You want it to be as close to stock as possible, especially if you're just starting out in karting. If the piston size is stock 0.005 or 0.010 inch oversize you should be O.K., but if it's 0.050 or 0.060 inch oversize you would be better off letting someone else buy it, unless the price is cheap and you want to use it for a backup or a parts engine. Generally, 0.035 inch is the legal maximum for IKF and WKA. Also 0.070 inch and larger pistons are very scarce. It is customary in the karting field to stamp the piston size or the amount it's oversize on the crown of the piston.

When checking the engine, carefully check the cylinder wall for gouge marks. The piston crown should be intact, and the piston ring or rings should be free in their grooves. Also inspect the engine for any external damage. Check the head for stripped spark plug threads. Check the exhaust header mounting bolts or inserts for any signs of stripping, and inspect the engine mounting flanges for cracks or broken out corners. If any of the above defects are found the engine should be priced accordingly.

Ask the seller if the carburetor is stock or if it has been modified in any way. If it's been drilled for alky you will have difficulty running gas. Refer to the section on Induction System Preparation to determine which type of carburetor you will need.

You should buy from someone you know, but that's not always possible. The only recourse you have is to ask the other karters about the seller. Try to find out how he's been running and how he treats his equipment. Remember it's your money.

When shopping for a kart look for a clean neat setup. This is usually an indication the kart has been well maintained

If your new to karting it's probably best to avoid unusual karts. I have to wonder how a kart like this will hold up to a couple of years of racing.

2-CYCLE THEORY OF OPERATION

This chapter contains the theory of operation for the major components used in karting. I have always found that it's easier to assemble or repair something if you have some understanding of how it operates. Hopefully, by placing this chapter ahead of the chapters on preparing and assembling your kart, you will have a better understanding of how it works and see the need for proper assembly.

The subjects covered are; the operation of the 2-cycle engine, spark plug fundamentals, the operating principles of the exhaust system, the operation of the magneto ignition system, and carburetion.

You should have some insight into each of these fields so you will be able to diagnose a problem when it arises. It's no longer enough to just get on the kart and drive it. You need to know how and why it works, and what to do when it doesn't.

I did not include the 4-cycle engine because it's covered in our book 4-Cycle Kart Engines and countless number of other books. This information is readily available at the local library. The 4-cycle engine operates along the same principle whether it's on a go-kart, lawn mower, garden tractor, or your car.

2-CYCLE ENGINES

The 2-cycle engine is the predominant engine used in karting today because of its fine power-to-weight ratio. Sometimes it's referred to as a two stroke. This engine receives its name from the fact that it fires on every revolution. The piston completes two strokes, one up and one down, with every revolution. This allows the engine to run at twice the RPM of a 4-cycle engine. The higher RPM allows the engine to develop more horsepower.

The 2-cycle engine is a very simple and straight forward engine, and has only three major moving parts; the piston, connecting rod, and the crankshaft. The following explanation and figures will give you a working knowledge of how the engine functions, so you can diagnose a problem if the engine refuses to run properly.

The engine depicted in the drawings is a reed valve engine, but the operating principles are alike, whether the engine has a reed valve, rotary valve, or piston port, induction system.

On the rotary valve engines the carburetor is mounted on the crankcase side cover so that the fuel inlet to the crankcase can be controlled by a rotary disc mounted on the crankshaft. The disc contains a window or cut out which opens the inlet port for a specified period of time. The crankcase pressure fluctuations are still required to draw the fuel into the crankcase.

The piston port engine has a crankcase inlet port cut directly into the lower half of the cylinder liner. The piston skirt itself actually opens and closes the port. As in the reed valve engine the engine crankcase pressure changes are still required to draw the fuel into the crankcase.

In most engines used in karting, the pressure changes in the crankcase are also used to

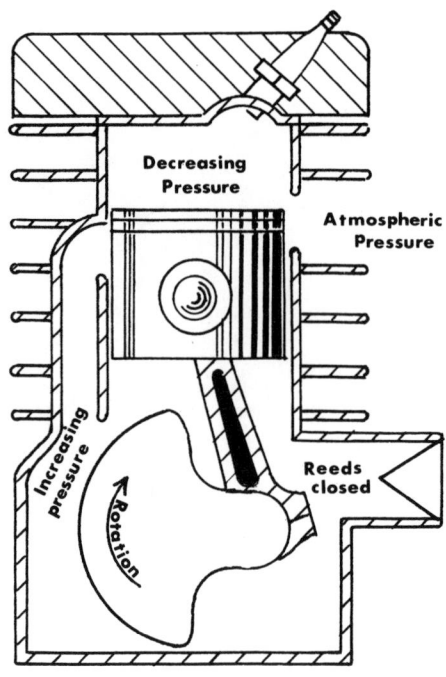

When the piston opens the exhaust port the brunt gases escape. The increasing pressure in the crankcase closes the reeds.

operate the fuel pump in the carburetor. This is more fully explained later in this chapter.

The necessary requirements for proper operation of the 2-cycle engine are spark, fuel, and an air tight crankcase seal.

The 2-cycle engine depends on the change of volumetric pressure in the crankcase to transfer the fuel from the carburetor, through the crankcase, and into the combustion chamber for firing by the spark plug. Without an air tight seal, the engine cannot perform properly. In the illustration(left), the piston is shown at approximately 22 degrees before top dead center (BTDC). Generally this position is where the timing is set to fire the spark plug. The plug is fired before TDC because it takes time, or a few degrees of rotation, for the flame front to progress across the combustion chamber and reach its peak effective power. If the plug is fired too early the power will operate against the rising piston causing a reduction of power. If the spark plug is fired too late in the cycle, the piston will have opened the exhaust port before maximum pressure is

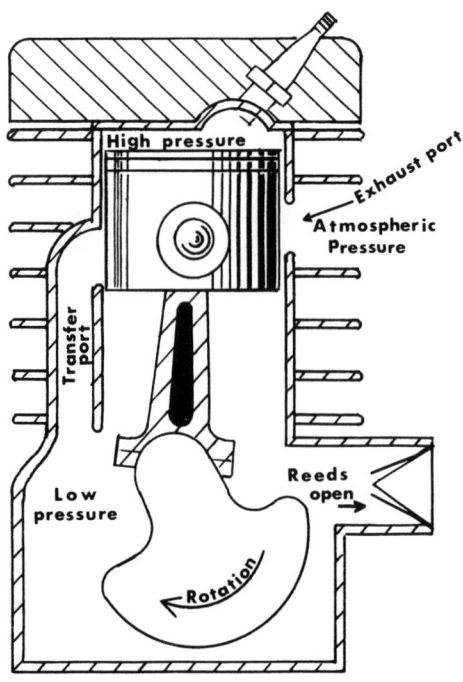

The piston is at 26 degrees BTDC. The area above the piston is at a very high pressure. A low pressure area is created in the crankcase, opening the reeds. The spark plug is ready to fire.

achieved, and all the energy would be exhausted out the exhaust port.

The energy created by the burning fuel mixture drives the piston downward with great force.

In the illustration Page 14 top), the downward traveling piston is shown opening the exhaust port. The spent energy in the combustion chamber is at a high pressure in comparison to the atmospheric pressure outside the exhaust port. A shock wave is developed. the spent gases exiting the cylinder cause a positive pressure wave to advance down the expansion chamber. The fast moving wave causes a low pressure area, or vacuum, to develop within the combustion chamber. At the same time this is happening, the piston is compressing the pressure in the crankcase. The crankcase pressure rises above the atmospheric pressure that is on the carburetor side of the reed valves. The reed valves are forced closed, sealing the crankcase and building the pressure even higher. A few degrees after the

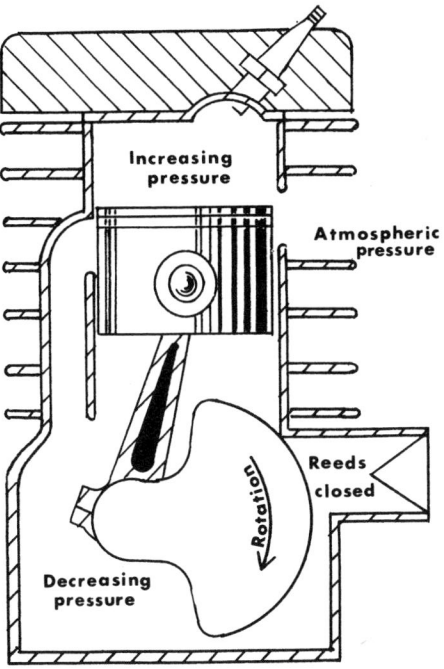

The piston now closes both ports and the compression builds again. The crankcase pressure decreases until the reeds open allowing a new charge of fuel to enter the lower chamber.

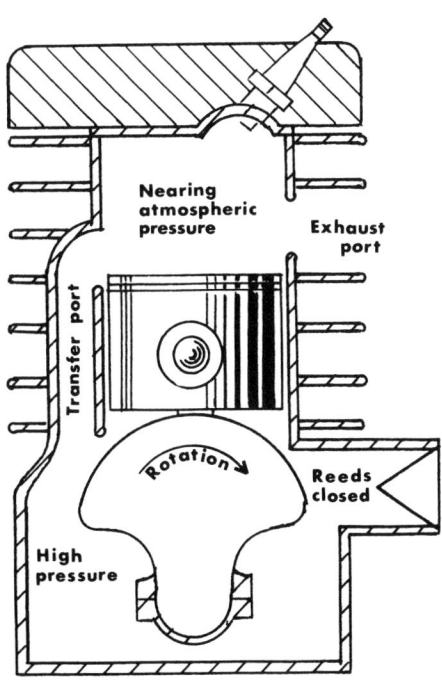

As the piston opens the transfer port, the high pressure in the crankcase transfers the fuel/air mixture to the upper cylinder.

exhaust ports are opened, the piston opens the transfer ports as shown in the following illustration. The upper cylinder is nearing atmospheric pressure while the crankcase is now at a high pressure, so the fuel mixture that is in the crankcase is pushed through the transfer ports and into the upper portion of the cylinder. The new charge will actually push the old burnt gases out the exhaust port since it is still open. Some of the new charge will also be lost, but the action of the tuned exhaust pipe will prevent this loss from becoming excessive.

In the next illustration, the piston has passed BDC and moved upward enough to close off the transfer ports and the exhaust port. The upward movement of the piston has created a vacuum or low pressure area in the crankcase. The atmospheric pressure on the carburetor side of the reed valves allow the reeds to open, thus permitting the new fuel mixture to enter the crankcase.

The upward moving piston compresses the fuel mixture until the plug fires again

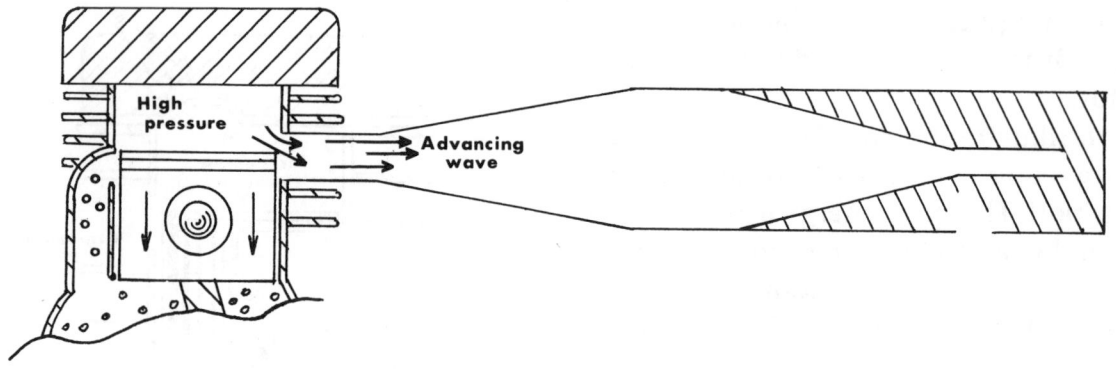

A shock wave is developed by the rapid opening of the exhaust port. The brunt gases travel down the pipe at the speed of sound.

starting the cycle all over again.

The importance of a tightly sealed engine is clearly shown. If an air leak occurs anywhere in the system, the required pressures cannot be developed and the engine will not perform properly.

EXPANSION CHAMBERS

The following is a brief explanation on the theory of the expansion chamber type of exhaust system. The exhaust system used in karting has enjoyed a great deal of development over the years, and has evolved into a very high performance system. The shape of the chamber may change somewhat from manufacturer to manufacturer, but the operating concept is the same. The main reason for the different shapes is an ever continuing attempt to make the usable power band as broad as possible. The usable power band can be moved higher or lower in RPM by adjusting the total length of the system. Some chambers are designed for good low RPM torque while others are designed for high RPM.

All new exhaust chambers used in karting today are equipped with silencers. The operation of the chamber is unaffected by the silencer. The silencer filters out the high frequency note of the exhaust, so that it will be less objectionable to the ear.

The volume of the expansion chamber is normally eight to twelve times the volume of the cylinder. Internally the chamber normally

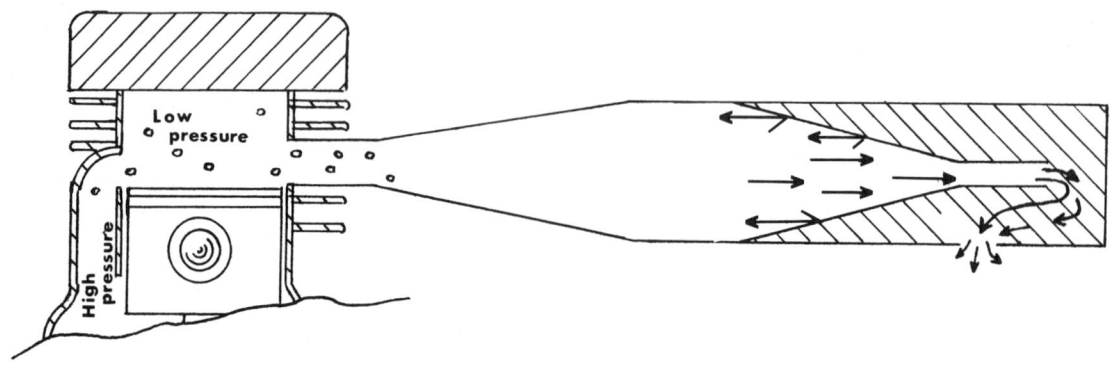

When the advancing wave reaches the restricted cone a portion of the wave is relected back to the exhaust port as a positive wave.

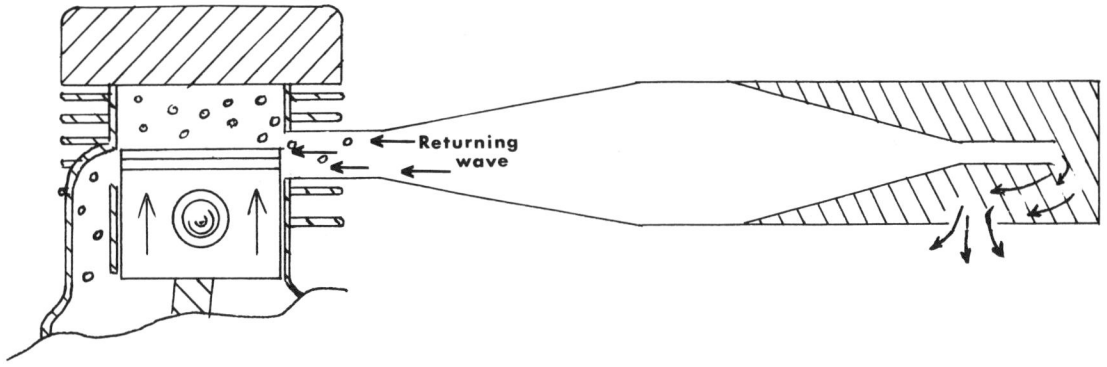

The returning positive wave returns the fresh charge that has escaped back to chamber. The piston is timed to close the port just as the exhaust gases reach the port returning them once again down the pipe with time to escape to the atmosphere.

contains no baffles. The exhaust action starts with the rapid opening of the exhaust port which creates a shock wave that travels down the exhaust pipe at the speed of sound, leaving behind it a negative wave or vacuum which reduces the cylinder pressure below atmospheric pressure as depicted in the illustration. Top of page 16. Meanwhile, the piston opened the transfer ports allowing a new fuel charge to flow from the high pressure of the crankcase to the low pressure of the cylinder. A part of this charge is actually drawn out of the exhaust port and into the flex pipe by the receding wave, see illustration bottom page 16.

While this is happening, the shock wave reaches the end of the expansion chamber and the restricted outlet acts as a partially closed end. A portion of the wave is exhausted to the outside atmosphere, but a portion of the wave is reflected back as a powerful positive wave. The return of this positive wave is timed by the length of the exhaust system so that it will arrive back at the exhaust port in time to push most of the extracted charge back through the port and into the cylinder as shown above.

The speed of the wave necessitates that the required length of the system may be as much as three feet, as measured from the exhaust port to the end of the stinger. This makes for a long exhaust system but countless hours of dyno testing have proved it necessary for increased horsepower and a broad, usable power band.

The expansion chamber is normally connected to the header by a small piece of flexible pipe. If the header works loose, or the flex develops a leak, some of the exhaust pressure will be lost and will not be available to return the extracted charge back into the cylinder. If the cylinder doesn't receive a full charge, the result will be a drop in output power. The difference between operating with an expansion chamber or an open exhaust is several horsepower. The difference between winning or finishing second is usually less than one horsepower.

The operating characteristics of the expansion chamber can be changed by adjusting the length of the flex pipe. If the flex is made very short the total length of the exhaust system is shorter and the exhaust wave will return to the exhaust port quicker. This means the combustion chamber will receive a full fuel charge at a higher RPM and consequently, the engine will perform better at high speed. However, some power will be lost at the low and mid-range area. If the flex length is lengthened, the exhaust wave will return to the exhaust port later. The combustion chamber will receive a full fuel charge at a lower RPM and consequently, the engine will have more torque and mid-range speed, but at some sacrifice of high end power. As you can see, the power curve of the engine can be adjusted by changing the flex length to suit the type of track you are running.

IGNITION SYSTEM

The most common type of ignition system found on small engines, is the magneto type. A pair of magnets generates an electrical current of relatively low voltage. The coil then transforms this voltage into the extremely high voltage necessary to jump the spark plug gap. The spark is timed to ignite the compressed fuel air mixture in the combustion chamber at the designated time.

For years machincal points were used to time the spark. Now days few engines still use machincal points. Almost all small engines now use some type of transistorized ignition system. In these types of ignitions the conventional points have been replaced with a solid state device, either a transistor or SCR. The reliability of these systems is greatly improved. The voltage developed with solid state devices is considerably higher, which improves the performance of the spark plug. The hotter spark reduces plug fouling.

The most common type of solid state system used in kart racing is the flywheel type. This means the flywheel carries the permanent magnets. As the magnets move under the legs of the coils a electrical current flows through the primary windings. The flow of current in the primary winding creates a very strong magnetic field surrounding the coil. At the moment of maximum current flow the transistor or SCR opens the circuit causing the magnetic field to collapse at a rapid rate. This induces a very high voltage in the secondary winding. This voltage is sufficient to jump the spark plug gap and ignite the compressed fuel air mixture in the combustion chamber.

The magnetic lines of force that are built up in the primary is directly related to the air gap between the coil legs and the flywheel. The coil should be set as close as possible without interfering with the rotation of the flywheel.

The timing of the spark is controlled by the location of a small trigger winding mounted on the coil. This means that the only way to adjust the timing is too rotate the coil around the flywheel. Most solid state systems are not adjustable.

The timing can be changed a very small amount by changing the air gap between the coil and the flywheel. The timing can also be changed by using offset flywheel keys but in most classes these are not allowed.

The Yamaha engine has a Transistor Controlled Ignition (TCI). It is similar to the type explained here.

Most foreign engines use the Motoplat Ignition. It is also a Electronic ignition but it is different mechincally. It has a series of coils and magnets mounted around the flywheel. It operates electrically the same as the one decribed above.

CARBURETOR

The diaphragm type carburetor is the most common carburetor used in karting today. The fuel pump has become a integral part of most carburetors. Unlike a automotive fuel pump, which is driven by a cam, the kart fuel pump is controlled by the pressure changes which take place in the engine crankcase. Most karting carburetors operate along the same principles, whether it's a Burris, Walbro, or Tillotson.

The fuel enters the pump via a fuel inlet valve and then passes through a screen filter which removes foreign particles from the fuel. The fuel then enters the fuel pump section of the carburetor. A diaphragm separates the chamber into two compartments; a fuel chamber and a air chamber. The air chamber is connected to the engine crankcase via a small hose. When the piston is on the upward stroke, the crankcase is below atmospheric

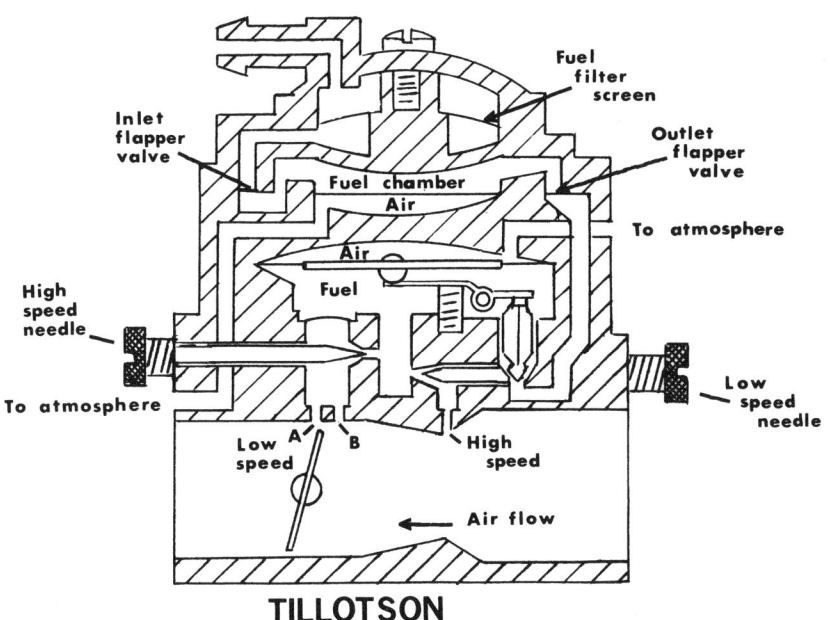
TILLOTSON

effect. In short, air flow increases speed as it passes through a restricted opening, the increase in speed causes a low pressure area behind it, which causes fuel to be drawn into the throat.

This causes the fuel to vaporize. Vaporization is required for efficient combustion. It's only the fumes or vapor from the fuel that burns, and not the liquid itself. The fuel will burn as a liquid, but only after ignition of the vapor increases its temperature.

You will note that the low speed passage has two, and in some cases three, discharge holes. When the throttle valve is closed, the engine is at idle and the fuel is drawn into the throat thru discharge hole A. Some air is actually drawn in thru discharge hole B and mixed with the fuel. When the throttle is partially open, the fuel is drawn through both discharge holes. At full throttle, almost all the fuel is metered by the main jet.

pressure. The low pressure or vacuum in the crankcase draws the fuel pump diaphragm down, thus opening the inlet flapper valve drawing fuel into the fuel chamber. When the piston is on the downward stroke, the engine crankcase pressure raises and the diaphragm flexes up closing the inlet valve and opening the outlet valve, allowing the fuel to enter the lower chamber. The lower chamber also has a diaphragm which divides it into two sections, a fuel and a dry chamber. The dry side of the chamber is connected to the crankcase.

In most 2-cycle carburetors crankcase pressure pulses are transferred to the air side of the lower chamber thru a internal passageway. As the crankcase pressure rises, the diaphragm forces the fuel inlet lever down, opening the fuel inlet valve and the fuel flows into the main fuel chamber of the carburetor. The fuel is then metered to the throat of the carburetor by the high and low speed needles. The fuel is vaporized by the passing air flow and carried through the reeds and into the engine.

The fuel is drawn into the throat of the carburetor by air flow through the throat. This action is called the venturi

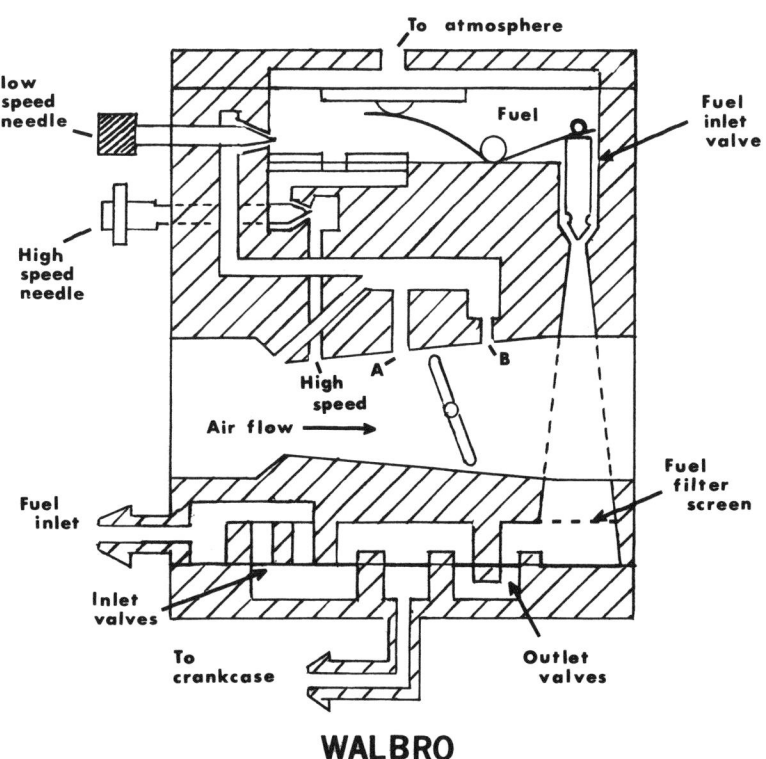
WALBRO

In some carburetors, the lower chamber dry side, is open to atmospheric pressure. When the engine is running the air flow through the throat causes a low pressure area at the orifice. The low pressure is then transferred to the fuel chamber, which combined with the atmospheric or higher pressure on the dry side, pulls the diaphragm down, opening the fuel inlet valve, allowing fuel to flow into the fuel chamber.

The Walbro carburetor used on the Yamaha engine, operates along the same principles as the other carburetors discussed in this section. However, there are a few minor differences. The fuel pump has a double set of inlet and outlet flapper valves. The fuel pump is still operated by pulses from the engine crankcase, but the pulses are carried to the carburetor by an external line. This line must be securely fastened at both ends to insure the crankcase seal is maintained.

SPARK PLUGS

The spark plug is really quite a simple device, and for the most part, is trouble free within itself. It's probably safe to say that most karters get less than adequate service from their plugs.

In racing, there is not only a selection of various heat ranges, but also a wide choice of plugs available.

The words "hot" or "cold" when used in reference to spark plugs are often a source of confusion since normally a hot plug is used in a cold engine. (low horsepower) and a cold plug in a hot engine (high horsepower). The terms actually refers to the plug's ability to transfer heat from its firing end into the engine cylinder head. The rating of the spark plug has little effect on the operating temperature of the engine, but is rather the range in which the plug itself will perform the best. A cold running plug, by definition, transfers heat rapidly from its firing end and is used to avoid overheating where combustion chamber or cylinder head temperatures are relatively high. A hot running plug has a much slower rate of heat transfer and is used to avoid fouling where combustion chamber or cylinder head temperatures, are relatively low.

Length of core nose and electrode alloy material are primary factors in establishing the heat rating of a particular spark plug design. Hot plugs have relatively long insulator noses with long heat transfer paths. Cold plugs have much shorter insulator nose lengths and thus, transfer heat more rapidly.

The spark plug is probably the most revealing component in the engine. The spark plug "sees" engine temperature very rapidly. With practice and proper magnification (4X to 6X power) plug firing end condition will pinpoint engine ailments and measure the condition and performance of a race engine. Properly interpreted a plug will indicate if a race engine is loafing or producing full horsepower. The spark plug will also reveal if the ignition system, timing, and carburetion, are correct.

Readings must be taken at maximum power output. It is imperative that the engine be shut off without choking the carburetor The ignition must be cut off at full power and the engine declutched with sufficient momentum to coast into the pits. A kart that is driven into the pits will erase all plug readings.

The following is a description of what to check for when reading spark plugs,

NORMAL
A normal plug will have sharp corners. The electrodes should not be discolored. The insulator nose should be white or very light tan. Very little discoloration should be present around the center electrode. A good plug can be cleaned and used again. Sandblasting of plugs is not recommended because it causes rounding of the edges. If the plug is to be used again, it can be cleaned with a wire brush.

FOULED:
A fouled plug will appear moist. The insulator nose and electrodes will be dark gray or black. The shell surfaces may contain a heavy build up of carbon deposits. If any of these conditions exist, the plug should be replaced.

OVERHEATED:
The electrodes will appear ash gray or milky white. Excessive pitting or traces of carbon deposits may appear around the center electrode. The insulator nose may be blistered or chalky white. The center electrode is rounded off at the edges. An overheated plug is most often caused by a lean fuel air mixture. The carburetor should be readjusted before internal damage results.

DETONATION
The exposed shell surfaces are speckled. Tiny pepper specks will appear on the insulator nose or electrodes. Excessive pitting or carbon deposits will also be in evidence. Tiny aluminum beads on the nose usually indicates metal is starting to leave the piston crown.

Whenever you install a new plug, be sure to set the gap. New spark plugs do not come with the gap preset. The gap should be set as recommended in the operators manual. The gap should be set with a wire type gauge. The round wire gauges are much more accurate than the flat feeler gauge types. When changing the spark gap, bend the side electrode only. Never try to bend the center electrode, as it will damage the plug.

When installing or removing the spark plug use the proper size socket, otherwise it may tilt and fracture the plug insulator. If the top of the spark plug has a screw on cap, it should be checked to insure it's tight, as they have been known to work loose and can cause the engine to misfire.

If you are going to run a modified engine or exotic type fuels you may need to change heat ranges. Talk to your engine builder or kart shop about which plug to use.

There is no trouble shooting for spark plugs. If you suspect it's bad replace it. If you don't think spark plugs are important I'll relate a true story. A coupe of years ago while in the pits at Indianapolis I observed George Bignotti reading the spark plugs from Gordon Johncocks Indy car. During the examination he invertially dropped one. He immediately threw all eight plugs in the trash can and put eight new ones in the car. How many times have you or I drop a plug and then put it back into our engine?

DETONATION

More racing engines, sustain power losses, are crippled by detonation, and are destroyed by preignition, than by any other engine abnormality.

A racing engine will not perform at peak power when in detonation. An engine cannot survive many races, even in a mild state of detonation, as the physical and thermal stresses inflict progressive damage to parts. Piston, spark plug, rod and bearing failures, and in many cases, blown head gaskets, can be traced to the engine being in a state of detonation.

Sustained detonation produces a general rise in temperature, with resultant weakening and removal of metal from the piston crown. Severe detonation is most likely to hammer a hole through the piston. The hole is usually sharp edged. Radial cracks, and a depressed area, may be found adjacent to the actual break. Evidence of excessive temperature can sometimes be seen in pitting on the top surface of the piston. Broken ring lands or cracks in the piston wall, may also be in evidence.

It is not all that uncommon to seize an engine without a rise in head temperature. This is a good indication of detonation. Detonation occurs when a portion of the fuel charge begins to burn spontaneously from the increased heat and pressures. This secondary flame front burns independently from the flame front produced by the firing of the spark plug. Detonation is the violent collision of these flame fronts within the cylinder.

Detonation is detectable by an audible, pinging sound, but it is normally not detected in practice or competition because it's drowned out by the roar of the exhaust.

If detonation is suspected, richen up the carburetor mixture, or retard the spark, or both. These measures may prevent engine damage until the cause is located. In some cases, detonation can be seen on a spark plug. Tiny pepper specks on the nose or electrodes. Fractured plug firing ends may also indicate detonation is occurring.

PREIGNITION

Preignition is ignition of the fuel charge prior to the timed spark. Any hot spot within the combustion chamber such as glowing carbon deposits, rough metallic edges, or overheated spark plugs, can be capable of initiating this combustion. As no orderly firing sequence occurs, the engine goes out of time.

Preignition destroys engines by heat, not by mechanical shock. The increase in heat occurs, on a piston and cylinder wall, when ignition occurs too early in the cycle. The intense heat can cause the piston to seize, break, or destroy the entire engine.

The piston is the most vulnerable part of a racing engine. It takes heat over the full surface of its crown but can pass heat only at its circumference. The heat must be transferred by the piston rings to the cylinder walls using two oil films as the conducting agent. The oil on the cylinder wall and the oil on the piston.

The extreme temperatures associated with preignition generally result in the melting of the piston. The edges of the break-through indicate a typical thermal failure unlike the mechanical failure caused by detonation, Spark plugs exposed to sustained preignition temperatures are likely to have their center electrodes melted.

Preignition can be caused by carbon deposits, or rough metallic edges in the combustion chamber, misadjustment of carburetor jetting, spark advance or an improper fuel/oil mixture.

An example of what detonation can do to a piston. The area around the hole, and at the top of the piston is rough and feels like sandpaper. Cracks can be seen around the hole. The hole is depressed. Note the broken ring land. The pressures inside the cylinder must have been tremendous.

4-CYCLE ENGINE THEORY

To fully understand how engines, carburetors, and exhaust system work, you need to understand what atmospheric pressure is and how it affects an engine. Atmospheric pressure is the weight of the surrounding air. While it may vary slightly from place to place and time to time, these variations are minor. As a rule this pressure is about 12 pounds per square inch. It is not important that you remember this figure, only that you realize that the atmosphere does exert pressure.

You can conduct a quick experiment of atmospheric pressure using a single sheet of paper. Pick it up by the top and you will notice that it hangs straight down. This is because the air pressure on both sides of the paper is the same. How place the flat of your other hand near the paper, without touching it. Swiftly move your hand away. You will observe that the paper will tend to follow your hand even though you did not touch it. That is because when you moved your hand away it created a low pressure area on that side of the paper. The higher atmospheric pressure on the opposite side of the paper pushed the paper into this low pressure area.

How that you have a brief idea of how atmospheric pressure works let's see how it applies to our engine. Pressure variations in an engine are created in two ways; First, by the movement of the piston. When the piston is moving downward in the cylinder it causes a low pressure (vacuum) above it. This is used to draw fuel into the cylinder. When the piston is moving upward a high pressure area is created above the piston. This high compression aids in fuel combustion. The second, way atmospheric pressure works in an engine is the venturi effect. This is used in the throat of the carburetor. It will be explained later in this chapter.

In order for a 4-cycle engine to run, four events must take place; First, it must intake a fuel/air mixture. Second, it must compress the fuel/air mixture. Third, it must ignite the mixture. and Fourth, it must exhaust the burned gases. Each of these events occurs during a stroke of the piston. A stroke is one upward or one downward movement of the piston. The engine makes two revolution to complete all four strokes. That is where we get the term 4-stroke, or 4-cycle engine. Let's look at these strokes more closely.

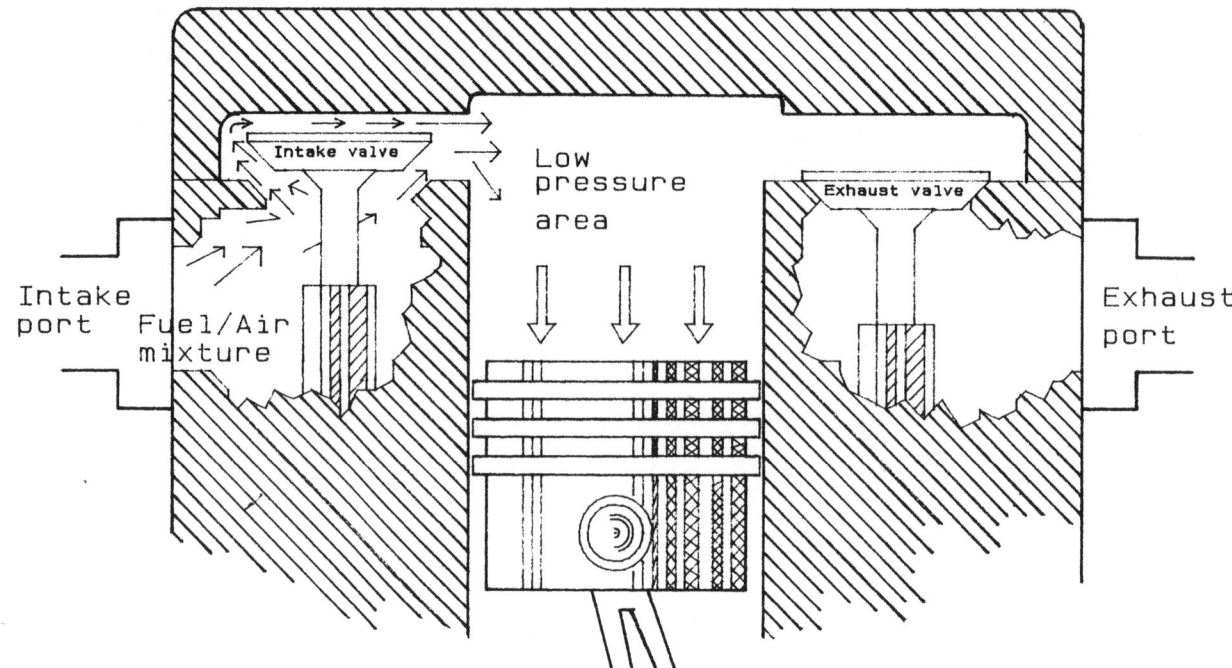

During the intake stroke the intake valve is open. The downward movement of the piston causes a low pressure area above the piston which draws the fuel/air mixture into the combustion chamber.

INTAKE STROKE

During the intake stroke the intake valve is open and the exhaust valve is closed. A low pressure area is formed inside the cylinder by the downward movement of the piston. This low pressure area or vacuum extends through the intake port into the throat of the carburetor. This vacuum pulls the fuel/air mixture into the combustion chamber through the open intake valve. After the combustion chamber is filled the intake valve will close and the compression stroke begins.

COMPRESSION STROKE

During the compression stroke the exhaust valve and intake valve are both closed. The fuel/air mixture has completely filled the upper cylinder, and the piston is starting it's upward movement, the fuel is compressed to a very high pressure. Just before the piston reaches the top of it's stroke the ignition system fires the spark plug beginning the power stroke. The spark plug is fired slightly before TDC (top dead center) because it takes time for a flame front too travel across the top of the piston and reach it's maximum power.

POWER STROKE

As the fuel burns the pressure in the combustion chamber increases forcing the piston downward. As the piston reaches BDC (bottom dead center) the exhaust valve opens for the exhaust stroke.

EXHAUST STROKE

The upward movement of the piston now pushes the burnt gases out the exhaust port. The plug will fire again at the end of this stroke but will not produce power because the exhaust valve is open and the cylinder is filled with burnt gases.

The intake stroke begins again and the cycles are repeated again as long as fuel and spark are available.

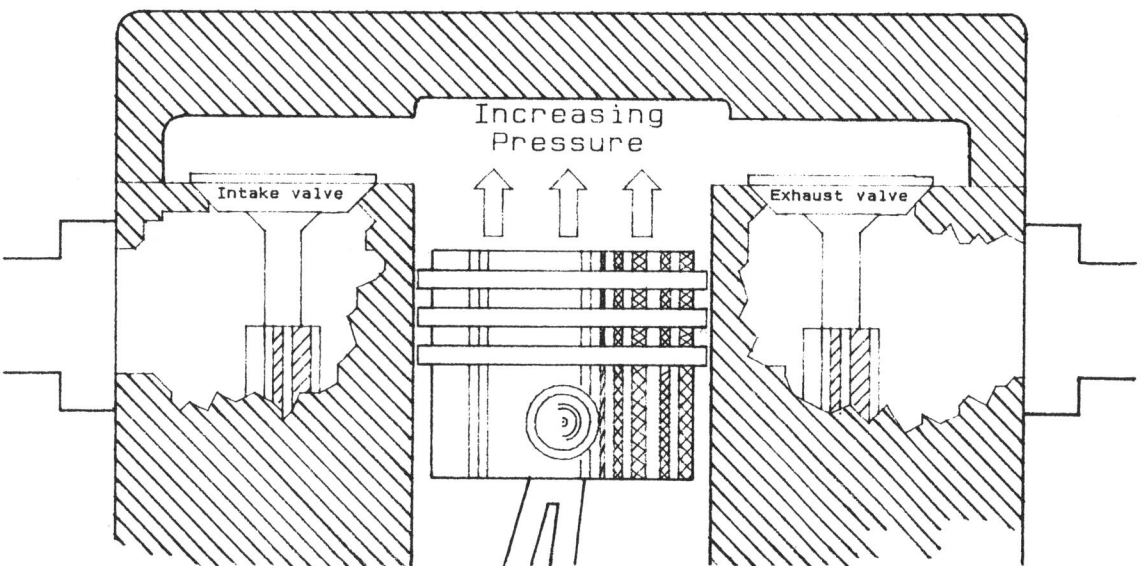

During the compression stroke both valves are closed. The rising piston compresses the fuel/air mixture. The spark plug fires near the end of this stroke.

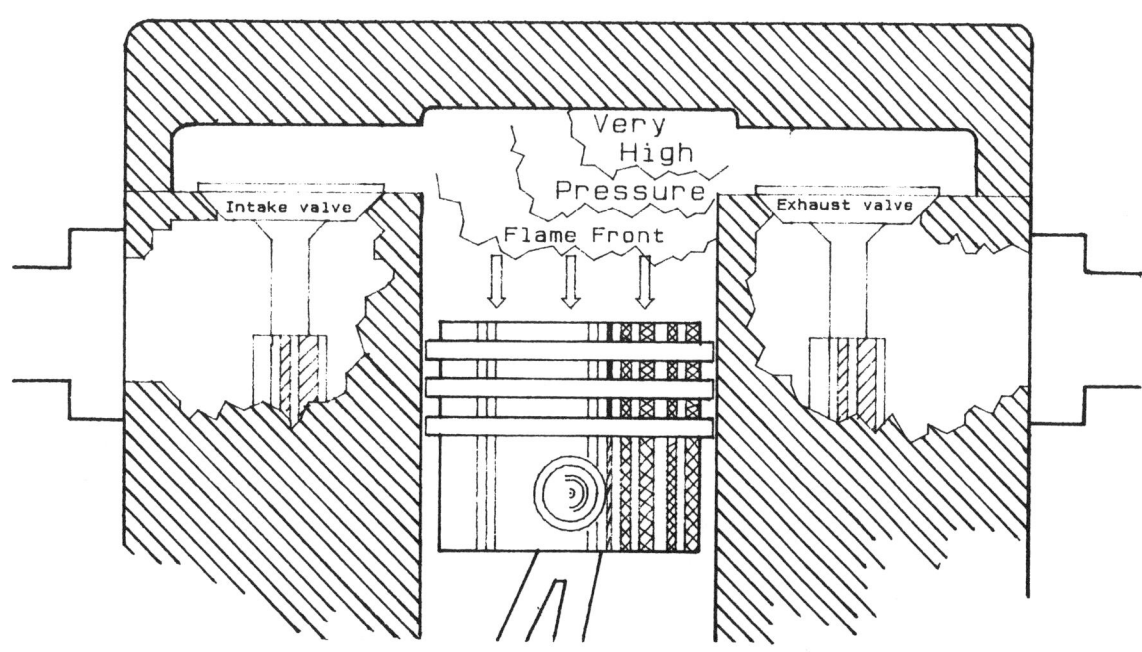

On the power stroke the burning air/fuel mixture generates a very high pressure which drives the piston down with great force.

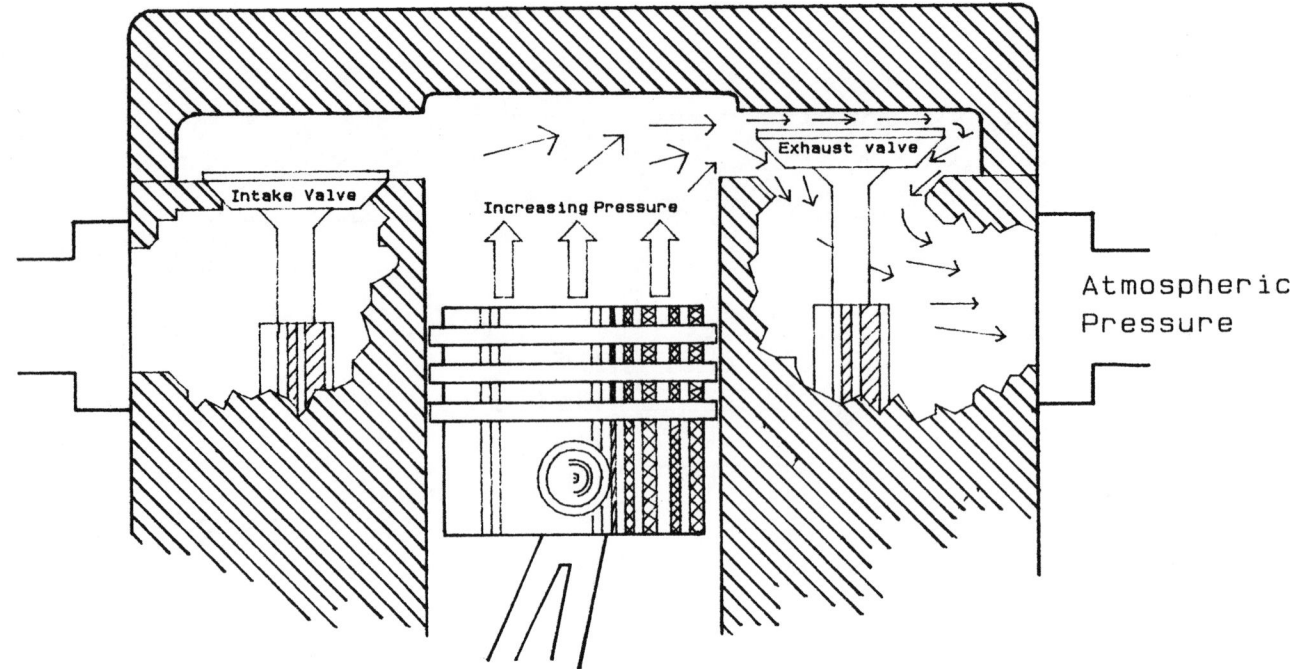

During the exhaust stroke the exhaust valve opens, allowing the rising piston to push the burnt gases into the exhaust system.

THE FLYWHEEL

Probably the most over looked item on the engine is the flywheel. Without it a multicylinder engine would run in a herky jerky manner, while a single cylinder engine would not run at all. When the piston reached bottom dead center it would simply stop and that would be that. To enable the engine to continue running a flywheel is mounted on the crankshaft. The flywheel is used to store some of the energy developed by the engine during the power stroke.

When the piston approaches bottom dead center the flywheel, being a large heavy mass, has picked up sufficient momentum to force the piston to continue back up the cylinder. This action is called reciprocating motion. That's why sometimes the 4-cycle engine is referred to as a reciprocating engine.

On each power stroke, energy is transmitted to the flywheel causing it to speed merrily along. Because of its mass it has ample momentum to rotate the crankshaft until the next power stroke. If there is none, the engine will coast to a stop. If the power stroke is repeated, the flywheels momentum will increase until maximum RPM is achieved.

The actual speed of the engine is controlled by the amount of power developed in the cylinder during the power stroke. This is controlled by the amount of fuel/air mixture entering the combustion chamber, which is controlled by the throttle, and we know who controls the throttle.

THE CARBURETION SYSTEM

I have used the Briggs pulsa-jet to explain how a carburetor works because it is the most common carburetor in 4-cycle karting. The Pulsa-Jet carburetor is unique to Briggs & Stratton engines. Most other manufacturers choose to use a float type carburetor. The Pulsa-Jet was designed for simplicity and ease of manufacturing.

It has become common for most carburetors to include a diaphragm type fuel pump. The pulsa-jet carburetor also incorporates a constant level fuel chamber. With this design very little fuel lift is required to draw fuel into the carburetor.

The name pulsa-jet comes from the fact that the engine creates a series of pulses which are used to operate the integral fuel pump. Actually the vacuum created by the piston works along with atmospheric pressure to pulse the fuel from the main tank into the fuel cup creating a pulsed fuel pump. The vacuum also draws the fuel from the fuel cup into the carburetor throat and ultimately into the combustion chamber.

Most carburetors have a restriction or narrowing in their throat called a venturi. When the air passes through the restriction its speed is increased. If a tube is inserted into the throat at this point the speed of the air will create a low pressure area at the base of the tube. If the other end of the tube is connected to a fuel supply the fuel will be drawn into the throat of the carburetor. A more detailed description of how the Pulsa-jet carburetor operates follows. Reference letters refer to illustration shown below.

During the intake stroke the piston creates a vacuum within the throat of the carburetor (h). The

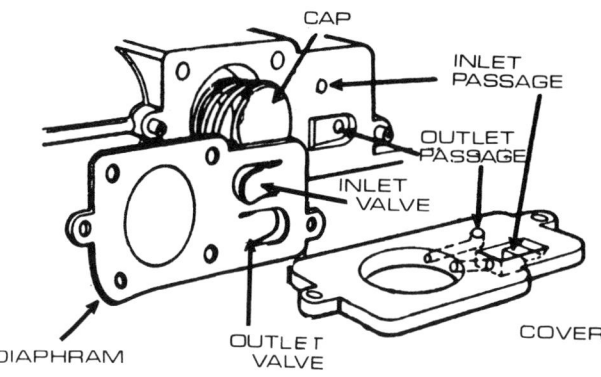

An exploded view of the Pulsa-Jet fuel pump. Note: it is mounted on the side of the carburetor.

vacuum pulls the diaphragm (b) and cap (a) toward the spring (c) compressing it. This movement creates low pressure area on the opposite side of the diaphragm, this is the fuel side of the chamber (g). This in combination with the atmospheric pressure within the fuel tank (you may have noticed a small hole in the top of fuel cap) pulls fuel up through the

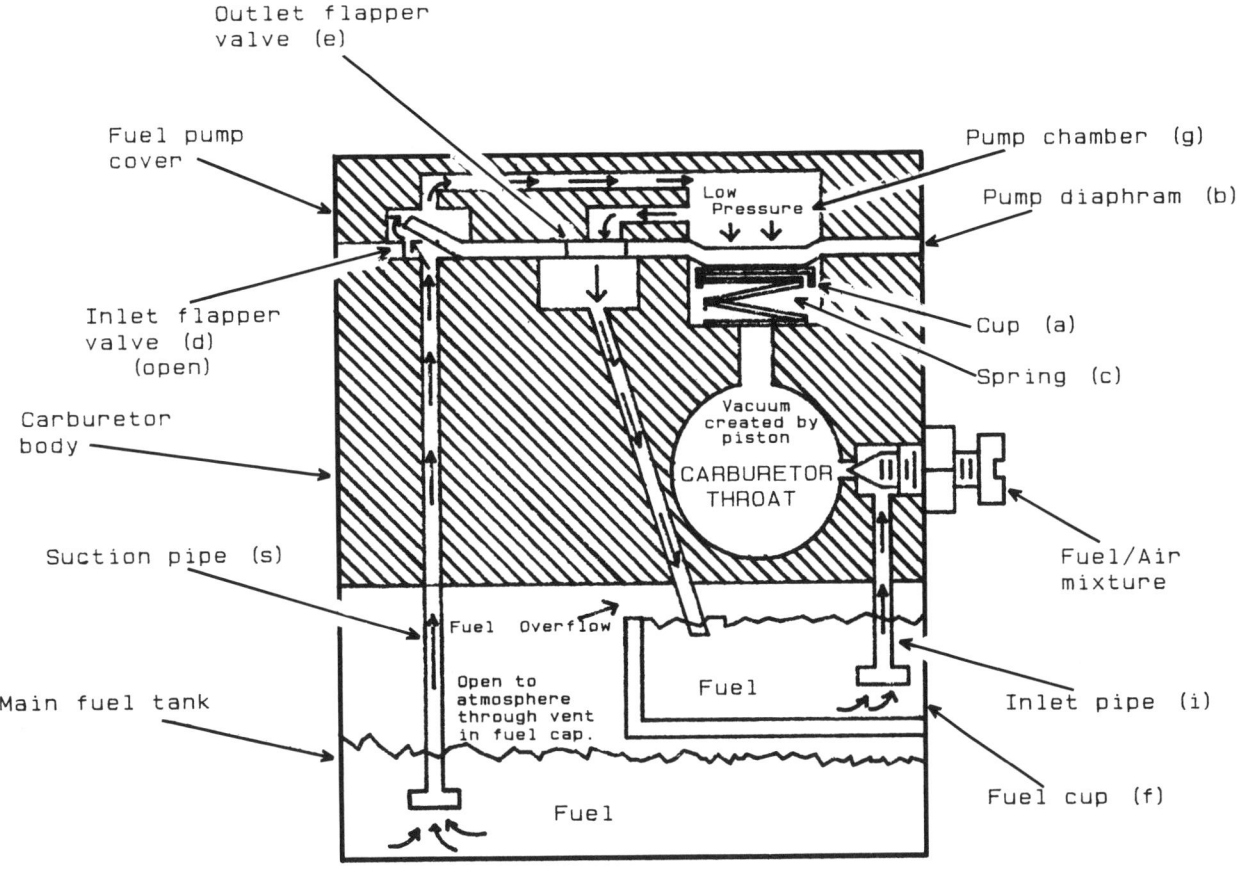

A cut away view of a typical carburetor with an integral fuel pump.

suction pipe (s). The pressure of the fuel opens inlet flapper valve (d) and closes the outlet flapper valve (e) filling the pump chamber (g) with fuel. When the piston begins its upward travel the vacuum in the throat is lost. This allows spring (c) to push the pump cap (a) and diaphragm (b) into the pump chamber (g). This causes the fuel in the pump chamber to close inlet valve (d) and open outlet valve (e). The fuel is pushed into the fuel cup (f).

The throat of the carburetor is connected to the intake pipe (i) which draws fuel from the fuel cup (f) into the throat of the carburetor. On the next intake stroke the cycle is repeated. This pulsation of the diaphragm keeps the fuel cup full. This fuel cup within the main fuel tank has openings at the top so that any excess fuel will overflow back into the main tank. A short fuel pick-up pipe (i) extends down into the small chamber. The purpose of this chamber within the tank is to reduce the amount of lift required and to insure that no matter how full, low, or tipped, the main tank is, there will be fuel available for the carburetor.

ELECTRONIC IGNITION

The solid state type of ignitions, of which the IC & Magnetron are, operate along similar lines. The only moving part is the permanent magnets mounted in the flywheel. There are no mechanical adjustment necessary. Some units do allow you to adjust the firing point. Solid state ignitions are not subject to wear, and they deliver uniform performance throughout their life. They are hermetically sealed against dust, dirt, oil, fuel and moisture.

A schematic of a simple electronic ignition system is shown here. When the magnets pass by the primary winding a low voltage is induced into it producing a magnetic field. A voltage is also induced into the trigger coil which is usually located near by. The trigger coil is so designed so that then the voltage reaches a certain level it will turn on or trigger the gate of the SCR. This is timed to occur when the voltage in the primary winding is nearing its maximum potential. When the SCR is triggered the field in the primary winding rapidly collapse inducing a voltage into the secondary winding. The coil is designed to step this voltage up very high. It may be as high as 30,000 volts. This voltage is sent to the spark plug where it is of sufficient level to jump the air gap between the electrodes of the spark plug and ignite the air/fuel mixture in the combustion chamber. This voltage is significantly higher than the standard point type ignition. In some systems such as the Briggs magnetron ignition the SCR is replaced with a special transistor, however, the basic operation of the system is the same.

In a solid state ignition system, the timing advance is controlled electronically by the voltage induced into the trigger coil. At slower RPM's it takes longer to build up the necessary voltage in the trigger coil to trip the transistor or SCR. At higher RPM the voltage is attained much more rapidly causing the timing to be slightly retarded. In the Briggs Magnetron ignition the engine will retard about 3 degrees as RPM increases.

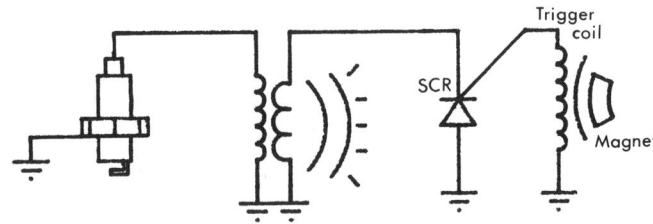

In a solid state ignition, the points have been replaced with an SCR(transistor). The SCR is turnd on or off by a trigger coil. When the rising voltage in the trigger reaches a certain level, it trips the SCR causing the primary field to collapse.

DRIVE SYSTEM PREPARATION

This section contains information on the initial preparation of the drive system. The principle function of the drive system is to transmit power from the engine crankshaft to the rear wheels. The drive system is made up of three major components, the clutch, sprocket and hub assembly, and the chain.

CLUTCHES

It's easy to become confused when discussing the clutches used in karting. There is: oil, dry, centrifugal and disc, just to name a few. Currently all the clutches used in karting are of the centrifugal type.

The disc clutches which have become so popular in the last few years is essentially a centrifugal clutch. Its operation does differ somewhat from the shoe and spring type clutches. In the disc clutch the centrifugal force acts on the weights which are mounted on a pivot pin securing them to the weight support plate. As centrifugal force is applied by the spinning crankshaft, the weight plate applieds pressure to the pressure plate and then to the fiber disc. There many be one, two, or three disc depending on the horsepower of the engine. Disc clutches have been used on motorcycles for many years. They are superior to the shoe type in high horsepower applications and are generally easier to adjust. They are also more expensive

The shoe or spring type clutch is much simpler than the disc type. When the engine idles, the weight of the shoes holds them close around the relatively slow turning crankshaft. As the crankshaft speed increases, centrifugal force throws the shoes out against the inner circumference of the drum, thus making the shoes and drum lock into one complete revolving unit. When the speed decreases the centrifugal forces lessen and the shoes disengage from the drum.

There is another variable in clutches, the oil clutch and the dry clutch. When first starting most karters end up using what ever clutch they acquire with their kart. There is no argument about the fact that the oil clutches

A disc clutch works by centrifugal force acting on a weight which works as a cam. When the heavy end of the weight is thrown out the smaller ear forces the pressure plate against the disc which in turn is forced against the drive hub. The action is the same whether the clutch has one, two, or three disc, or is a dry or an oil clutch.

are superior to the dry type. If you are running a dry clutch, in a class that allows oil clutches you should spend the money for a oil clutch. The oil clutch has become popular in kart racing because it allows the shoes to slip somewhat during engagement and disengagement, avoiding the sudden loading of the engine which tends to cause severe bogging when the kart is coming out of the corners of the track. This maintains the engine RPM in its most effective range, and allows the driver to use his brakes to control the kart through a corner while blipping the throttle to keep up the engine RPM. The slipping clutch permits this, and will allow the kart to come out of the turns much faster than the dry types. In an effort to control cost some classes require the use of a dry clutch.

With a new clutch, it's important that it be broken in properly. With most clutches you will receive a sheet with the manufacturers break-in procedure, follow it. If you don't have one follow this procedure. This procedure is good for oil or dry clutches. You should have most of the weights supplied with the clutch, mounted for the break-in period. The purpose of this is to prevent overslipping. Overslipping will cause the fiber linings to glaze, or in the case of steel shoes, the shoes will score. Take the kart out on the track and run a few laps at a moderate speed. When properly adjusted, the clutch should slip just a little coming out of the turns. With all the weight on the clutch it probably will not slip. Gradually start removing weight until the clutch just starts to slip. Always remove a equal amount of weight from each shoe. The clutch must always be balanced.

The shoes must be equally spaced around the hub no matter how many shoes are used.

The shoes and drums should be inspected occasionally for wear. Fiber linings should be replaced before they wear down to the rivets, or the drum may be damaged. Steel Shoes should be replaced if more than 50 percent of the shoes are worn. The drum should be replaced if its inner surface becomes out of round or scored. Disc should be replaced if they become worn or glazed.

If your clutch uses springs for tension, start with a light spring and work heavier. I can't tell you which spring or how much weight to use because it depends on driver/kart weight, engine, and track. If you run more than one track you will most likely have a different setup for each track.

Clutches are available as inboard and outboard models. This refers to the location of the drive sprocket on the drum. If the teeth are

HORSTMAN DISC CLUTCH

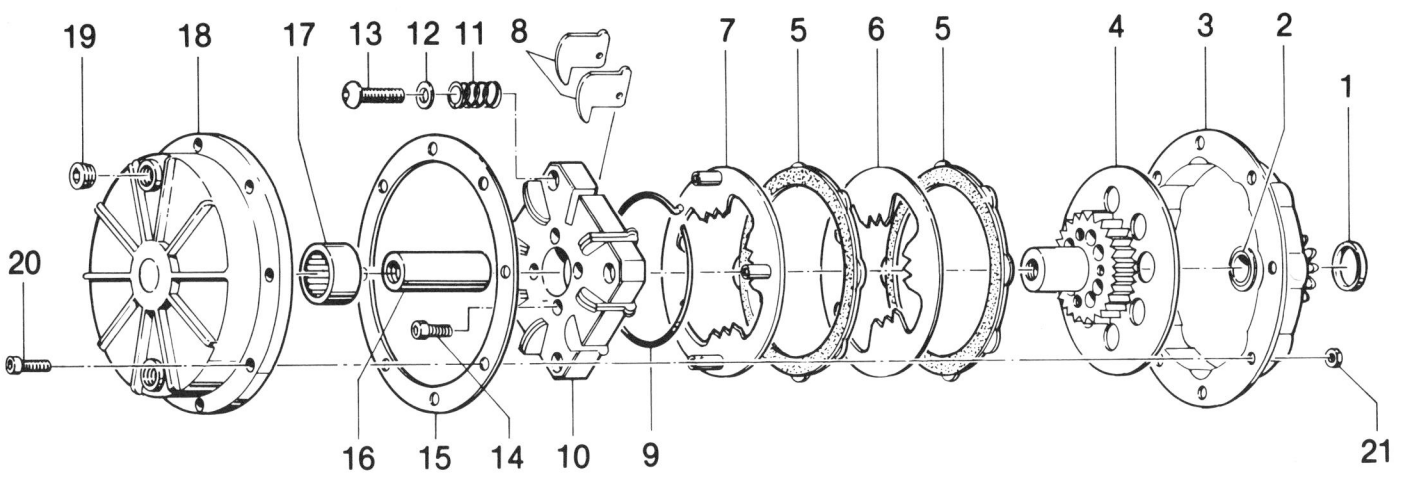

PARTS LIST

ITEM NUMBER   **DESCRIPTION**

- 0   Complete Clutch
  (*Specify number of teeth on drum)
- 1   Spacer, .125" wide, use with 9T drum
  Spacer, .125" wide, use with 10T thru 15T drums
- 2   Bushing for 9T drum
  Needle Bearing for 10T thru 15T drums
- 3   Drum with 9 tooth sprocket
  Drum with 10 tooth sprocket
  Drum with 11 tooth sprocket
  Drum with 13 tooth sprocket
  Drum with 14 tooth sprocket
  Drum with 15 tooth sprocket
- 4   Drive Hub
- 5   Lining Disc
- 6   Floater Disc
- 7   Pressure Plate
- 8   Weights, cam action
- 9   Weight Guide Ring
- 10   Aluminum Activator Plate
- 11   Compression Spring
- 12   Washer
- 13   Screw, button head
- 14   Screw, soket head, 10 - 32 x 3/8" long
- 15   Gasket
- 16   Starter Nut
- 17   Bearing
- 18   Oil Cover with Bearing
- 19   Plug, oil fill
- 20   Screw, socket head, 8 - 32 x ½" long
- 21   Nut, 8 - 32

> This is a typical disc clutch. The clutch is basically the same whether it's a 2-cycle or 4-cycle, oil or dry type.

Presented courtesy of Horstman Mfg., Inc.

NORAM/RATECH 4-CYCLE CLUTCHES

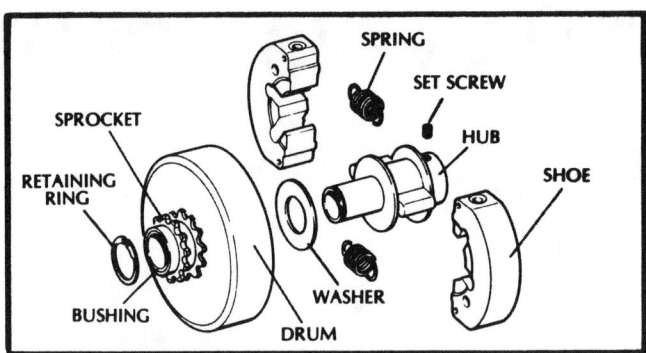

There are several different models of steel shoe clutches used in karting. Generally they are of the same basic design. They are often referred to as Noram clutches as they where originally sold. Today Racing Technology Corp. (RATECH) produces most of this type of clutch. These clutches are popular because of their smaller size and simple operation. It's simply centrifugal force forcing two metal shoes out against a steel drum.

As simple and straight forward as they are, there is quite a bit of adjustment range. The clutch engagment speed is adjustable in three ways. By using different weight shoes, by using different tension springs, and by the shoe mounting location.

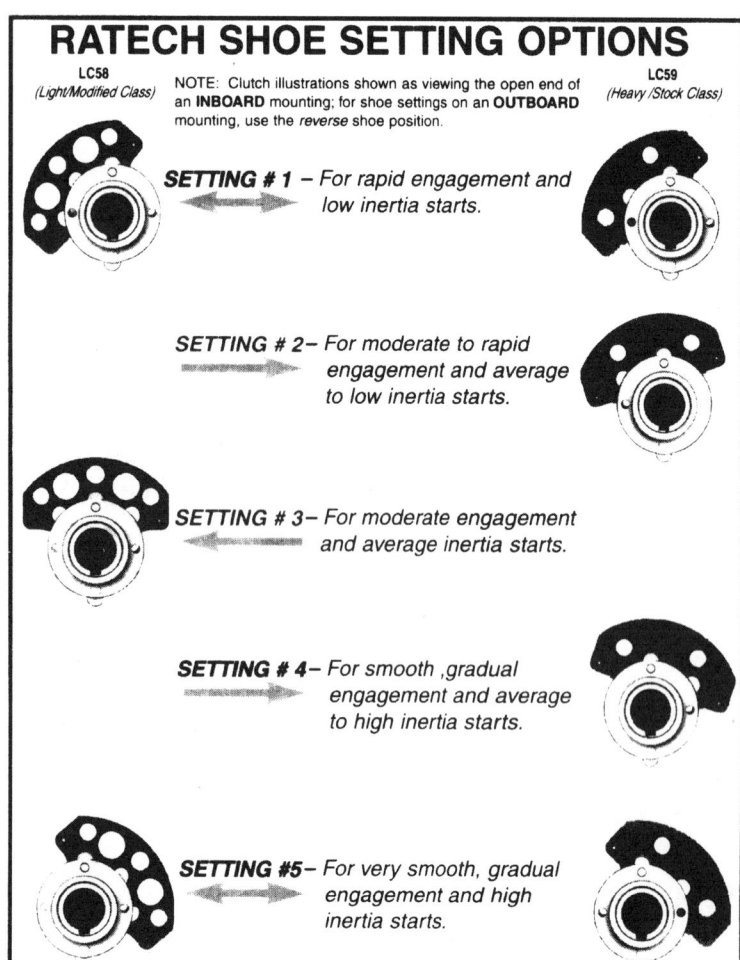

Shoes are available in several different weights. You can tell the approximate weight by the holes drilled through the shoes. The springs which secure the shoes are also available in various sizes. The springs are color coded so you can tell the difference. The shoes location on the hub also affects the type of engagement.

SPRING COLOR	ENGAG. SPEED W/LIGHT SHOE	ENGAG. SPD. W/HVY. SHOE
Orange	1210	1035
Yellow	1300	1110
Brown	1520	1300
Black	1780	1520
Red	2050	1755
White	2340	2000
Blue	2620	2240
Purple	3500	2990
Green	4000	3420
Orange	4500	3900
Brown	5000	4300
Red	5500	4730

Presented courtesy of
Racing Technology Corp.

located between the engine and the clutch, it's an inboard. If the teeth are located on the outside, away from the engine, it's an outboard.

If you have a choice, the inboard type is preferred. It's better for the load, the load is the torque required to move the kart forward, to be placed on the crankshaft, close to the engine where, the crankshaft bearings can help support the load. The outboard models tend to place the drive stresses out on the end of the crankshaft where there is no bearing to help support it.

In the Yamaha and open classes it has become common to use a third bearing support on the PTO end of the crankshaft to help alleviate this problem. This is a very good idea, however is it an added expense.

Some drums have a bronze bushing type bearing pressed into them. These bearings do become worn. You can tell by sliding the drum on the crankshaft. It should fit without wobbling. The bearing can be pressed out, and a new one carefully pressed back into place. The bearing is available at most any kart shop. After installation, the bearing may need to be reamed out with a reamer. Check for a proper fit BEFORE assembling the clutch.

The drum is sealed with a gasket (Horstman and Burco clutches) which should be replaced if the clutch begins to leak. A leaking clutch can cause oil to be sprayed on the rear tire and cause the kart to become uncontrollable.

The clutch is one thing the beginning karter tends to shy away from, so a few hours of practice with a friend, and a stopwatch, can give you an edge on some of your competitors come race day.

Some direct drive systems are starting to appear. Direct drive has never been very popular in the United States. Direct drive is somewhat faster on the larger courses but is not quite as good on slow tight courses. Direct drive karts generally are very awkward to start. I don't recommend it for a beginner.

CLUTCH OIL

On the subject of clutch oil, follow the manufacturers recommendations. Clutch oils can be very expensive, but they are specially formulated for the job they perform. The oil is specially engineered for extreme temperature and pressure and most contain antifoaming characteristics and special slipping agents. These help provide consistent performance.

To get your moneys worth, buy the brand recommended for your clutch. The oils function is to provide slipping, to prevent engine booging, and cooling. Adding more oil than recommended will not increase the amount of slipping. If the clutch is not slipping, weight should be remove or the clutch adjusted. Clutch oil is expensive, there is no need to waste it.

When filling or adding oil, remove both filling screws if your cover has two, so the air can escape. Turn the clutch so that one hole is at 10 O'clock and the other at 4 O'clock. Fill from the top hole slowly until the oil just begins to run out the bottom hole. You can rock the clutch to help the air to escape. This is necessary if your clutch cover has only one fill hole.

Clutch drums are available with several different sprocket sizes. Almost all 2-cycle sprint racers use a drum with a 9 tooth sprocket. The karters running in the 4-cycle or speedway division may use a 12 tooth or larger sprocket.

A lot of karters get into figuring gear ratos. If you want to know the rato O.K., but the real truth is you only need to determine which gear works best for you and that can only be determined with a stop watch, no matter what the rato is. Unless you have a lot of various size clutch drums which you intend to switch back and forth the ratio means little. The only real reason you would need to know the ratio is if you wanted to make a change and you didn't have any smaller, or larger, sprockets. You would then be forced to change the clutch drum. Knowing the ratio you were using before would allow you to know which tooth sprocket to change the axle sprocket too.

Axle clutches have been on the market for several years now, but they have not become popular in the sprint classes. They are used almost exclusively in the Enduro division and are not covered here.

CLUTCH INSTALLATION

Some of the older clutches required a spacer between the engine and the clutch. About the only way to find out if you need one, is to mount the clutch, tighten the clutch nut and a couple of the drum bolts, and then check the end play. Grab the clutch, then push and pull toward the engine. If it has enough play for the spacer, it should be used. If it's not used the excessive end play will cause undue wear on the clutch sprocket and the chain. When installing the clutch hub of shoe type clutches, be sure that the shoes are mounted in the proper direction. The shoe must trail the clevis pin. The rotation of the engine must be able to throw the shoes out toward the drum. Insure that the crankshaft key stays in the keyway, if the clutch is a keyed unit. When the clutch hardware has been tightened, check to see that the drum will spin freely without turning the engine over. If it binds up, you will need to disassemble the clutch and locate the problem. It's always a good idea to add the clutch oil now, so that it's not over looked later. It will also give you a chance to see if the unit leaks. If the clutch leaks, replace the damaged gasket or bushing. If you don't, oil may be splashed on the rear tire during the race causing you to spin out. Be sure to properly torque the clutch nut.

CHAIN

Chain, what can go wrong with a chain? You buy it, put it on and forget it. Wrong, one of the highest causes of DNF (did not finish) is chain problems.

It doesn't matter who you ask about a chain you'll, get a different answer. It doesn't matter which brand you use as long as you use a brand name. Chain failures themselves are rare. The biggest cause of chain failure is sprocket misalignment or a rear axle that walks during cornering. Just remember, a good chain will only last as long as you maintain it properly.

Karting has adopted the standard No. 35 chain. No. 35 chain is also used on minibikes. The motorcycle industry has adopted No. 40 chain for its final drive. They are not interchangeable. In recent years we have seen the introduction of belt drives and #219 chain which is currently used on Horstman axle clutches.

One of the more popular space type chain should be used. They are superior to the standard No. 35 chain. It has extra space between its plates to reduce friction in this area.

LUBRICATION

Proper and sufficient lubrication not only minimizes metal to metal contact, but provides effective cooling and impact damping at high speeds.

There are many lubricating oils on the market today which are more than adequate. I personally prefer the new spray can oil developed for the motorcycle industry. The new foam types are not supposed to fly off during operation. They slowly seep into the crevices where it's really needed.

CHAIN BREAKERS

With some chains you buy today, you will receive a master link for assembling your chain. The master link comes with various styles of locking plates: spring clips, wire locking, and cotter keys. In my opinion, your best bet here is to throw them all away. The master link is always the weakest link in the chain and it'll give out just when you least want it to. For a few dollars you can buy a good chain breaker. There are several different types on the market, most of them are of the motorcycle variety or adaption there of.

Most of these types were originally designed for the larger motorcycle size chains, and if not used properly, the lip which holds the chain in place will break. If you receive an instruction sheet with your breaker read it, it only takes a minute to figure out the proper way to use the tool. I think the type shown here is by far the best of whats available. It has practically nothing to break and should last forever. I have used one for nearly twenty years. You should be able to get one from your local kart shop. They are well worth the money.

One of the better type chain breakers. I have used the same one for twenty years.

SPROCKETS

There are two major manufacturers of wheel sprockets; Horstman and Azusa. The sprockets are made to fit standard size hubs and both are of the split design. It does not matter which brand you buy. The sprockets do come in different thickness 0.125 and 0.160.

The only difference that is important to the karter is the marking for proper alignment. Due to the split design, it's necessary to properly align the two halves when installing the sprockets on the hub. Horstman sprockets have a slash mark to indicate the matching ends. The slash marks must be butted together for proper mating. Azusa sprockets have a special washer which fits on the two mounting bolts at the split. It's not necessary to use the washer, however the recess provided for it indicates the mating ends.

The drive hub on the rear axle should be inspected to see if it's cracked or broken. If any of the sprocket mounting bolts are stripped, they should be replaced. If the hub is one of the Heager spin on types, it's a good idea to remove the retaining ring and clean the threads on the hub, and on the ring and coat them with light oil.

The sprockets themselves should be inspected to insure they are flat. The best way to do this is to lay it on a known flat surface such as a piece of pane glass. If the sprocket is on the kart spin the axle and check for side wobble. Check all your sprockets while your at it.

Inspect the sprocket for missing teeth or excessive wear. If the teeth on the sprocket or clutch drum shows excessive wear, or have broken or missing teeth, they should be replaced. Damaged teeth will cause slop in the chain and subject the rollers to unnecessary abuse, which leads to cracking, and if not corrected, total chain failure. Any damaged sprockets should be discarded. They cannot be satisfactorily repaired.

SPROCKET ALIGNMENT

Sprocket alignment is one thing which can be very aggravating to achieve with the older taper collared hubs. The newer one piece hubs have made alignment much easier.

Sprocket misalignment is easy to spot because one side of the teeth will usually show excessive wear. If properly aligned, you should be able to lay a straight edge along the teeth of the axle sprocket, and it should align with the sprocket on the clutch.

CHAIN ADJUSTMENT

After the sprocket has been properly aligned the chain can be installed. Proper adjustment is very important to proper operation of the chain. The chain should not be adjusted tight. A tight chain will put undue stress on the engine crankshaft and clutch bearings. If the chain tightens more during a race, it will have no recourse but to break the chain or maybe worse yet, the crankshaft. A chain should not tighten during the race. If it does it should be replaced. A chain starts tightening because of insufficient lubrication or external damage such as dropping a wheel off the track and driving on the sprocket and chain. Once a chain begins to kink, it cannot be successfully repaired. It will only get worse. There should be about 1/4 inch of slack in the chain. Care must be used here to prevent the chain becoming too loose, or else the axle may flex under stress and pop the chain off. A loose chain also causes a snapping action every time you apply power, which will quickly break most any chain.

Check to insure that the chain is not stretched or twisted. If you have thrown the chain it is not uncommon for it to be stretched. One way to check for this is to spin the rear wheel by hand. If it tightens up in some spots and loosens in others it's a good indication the chain is stretched. The chain can also become twisted. You should be able to see this while looking for a stretched chain.

Lay a straight edge along the teeth of the axle sprocket, it should align with the sprocket on the clutch.

There should be about 1/4 inch of slack in the chain. A tight chain will put undue stress on the engine crankshaft and clutch bearings.

INDUCTION SYSTEM PREPARATION

The principle function of the induction system is to move the fuel from the fuel tank through the carburetor and into the engine. The major component of the induction system is the carburetor. Carburetor disassembly and reassembly is discussed. Pressure checking the carburetor is also explained.

A portion of this chapter is devoted to fuels and the various types used such as; gas, alcohol, no-lead, low-lead, and white gas. The proper carburetor for the proper fuel is also discussed. How to mix the proper fuel/oil mixture, premixed fuel, and flushing the carburetor after a day of racing, is also explained.

CARBURETOR

The carburetor seems to mystify most rookies, but it's really not that difficult to understand. The carburetor is basically a small diaphragm type fuel pump, which then mixes the fuel with air and feeds it to the engine. Every karter should know how they operate, and now to rebuild his carburetor. It is necessary to inspected and clean them occasionally.

DISASSEMBLY

This procedure was written for the Tillotson carburetor. However, most all carburetors used in karting are similar in construction and operation. Remove the top mounting screw and lift the top cover from the body. On the under side of the top you will find a fuel inlet filter screen. It should be cleaned thoroughly. Remove the 6 fuel pump body screws, and remove the fuel inlet body. Inspect the fuel pump diaphragm. Removal of the fuel pump body will reveal a flapper valve, type of diaphragm. Next remove the diaphragm cover to reveal the fuel pump diaphragm itself. Inspect the diaphragm for cuts, tears, or holes. If it's punctured, it will not pump properly, and will require replacement. The diaphragm should be flexible. If it becomes hard or brittle it should be replaced. To inspect the fuel inlet needle remove the screw that holds the inlet lever pin. The inlet valve is held between the two fingers of the inlet lever, or fulcrum arm, as it's sometimes called. Note the little spring beneath the lever, becareful not to lose it. Inspect the needle and its seat for wear.Reinstall the fuel inlet needle, be sure to include the spring. Tighten the screw snug and check that the lever moves freely. To adjust the fulcrum arm, use a straight edge and set the arm until it is flush with the top of the body. Carefully bend the fingers of the arm up or down to obtain this setting. When you have the arm adjusted, push it down and insure that the fingers of the arm lifts the inlet needle slightly. Also check to insure that the needle closes.If the valve is not allowed to close, fuel will pass through the high speed needle continuously,and you will be unable to properly adjust the low speed needle. This is a approximate setting and you may wish to change it after some track testing. When reassembling the carburetor, The gaskets should be replaced. There are gaskets sets available. The gaskets should be changed at least once a year. The diaphragm will become brittle after a time, and will not pump properly. Install the cover plate and tighten the mounting screws. Do not overtighten or the carburetor will not seal properly.

The carburetor can be pressure checked the same as the engine. It can be done on or off the engine. Connect the pressure checker to the fuel inlet port. Slowly pump the pressure up to about 5 pounds. If you pump the pressure higher it will overcome the pop off pressure of the fuel inlet spring, and allow the air to escape into the throat of the carburetor.

A gas carburetor with a stock spring has a pop off pressure of about 10 pounds but a alcohol carburetor can have a pressure as low as 5 or 6 pounds. The carburetor should hold 5 pounds pressure for four or five minutes. If the carburetor will not hold pressure, it may be because the fulcrum arm is set too high and will not allow the fuel inlet valve to close. The arm should be readjusted to a lower setting. The problem could also be the gaskets are not seating properly. You may need to lap the gasket surfaces to get a good seal. To lap the gasket surfaces, lay a piece of emery cloth on a flat surface. Move the piece to be trued back and forth on the emery cloth. This will give you a smooth, flat surface.

Inspect the high and low speed needles for proper hardware. The spring, flat washer and the rubber 0-ring, must be installed correctly for the needle to perform properly.

FUELS

The two basic types of fuel used today are gasoline and methanol. It is also possible to use a mixture of these, or to purchase one of the several premixed fuels on the market. Most of the rookie classes are gas only classes, but you will find that all of the advanced classes allow the use of other fuels. If your class allows premix or methanol you will have to use it, to be competitive. For the new karter, it would be a good idea to start with gas, at least for the first couple of weeks. It's somewhat easier to make the carburetor adjustments because the settings are not quite so exacting. This will allow you more time to spend with other things. After you become accustomed to making carburetor adjustments while the kart is in motion, you can switch to methanol.

GASOLINE

When running gas, you should use high-test leaded gas. It is still available if you hunt for it. Although it is becoming scarce and may soon become unavailable. The purpose of buying high test is to get a fuel with a high octane rating. Do not buy no-lead, low-lead or white gas. These gasses will not burn clean in todays high powered kart engines. They can cause preignition and will almost always destroy a piston. This is especially true of a modified, or high compression engine. Premium fuel is becoming harder and harder to find. If you must use a regular grade fuel, it will be necessary to add octane booster to prevent preignition and detonation.

The octane rating should be increased to about 95 or 97, follow the directions on the label. You may have noticed that the octane rating of premium has also been lowered somewhat in the last few years. In the near future, it may become necessary to add booster to premium. If all else fails we will all have to switch to methanol, or one of the premixed fuels.

When purchasing octane booster, be sure you know what you are buying. Read the label closely. Most automotive supply houses carry some type of gas booster or octane additive. Most of these are mineral based and will not mix with methanol. If you are running a fuel containing methanol, you must use a non-mineral base booster, such as Klotz.

If you are going to participate in WKA and IKF sanctioned races in a gas only class you must be very careful how much octane booster you add, or you may fail the fuel test. Some tracks tech fuel by measuring its specific gravity. Octane booster will raise the specific gravity of gas. The best way to protect yourself. Is to wait until you arrive at the track. Have your fuel pretested, and then add booster in small amounts till you reach the proper legal limit.

Gasoline is not always the same. The refineries change the ratios of the additives depending on the seasons of the year, In the fall of the year, it is not uncommon for some pump gases to fail the specific gravity test straight from the pump.

OCTANE

What is Octane? Octane is the anti-knock performance of gasoline. If it's too low for a given engine, it will knock. Knock is a high pitch, metallic, rapping noise. In severe cases, knock may lead to uncontrolled preignition. Octane does not add horsepower, and if you buy a good grade of premium, adding additional octane booster will be of no value.

There are presently two methods of determining the octane number; the motor method and the research method. The SAE (SOCIETY OF AUTOMOTIVE ENGINEERS) has introduced an anti-knock index which is a combination of both motor and research methods. The anti-knock index is more closely related to actual road anti-knock performance and is the number most often found on gas station pumps. The index number of premium gasoline is about 97, while regular grades are about 89, unleaded fuel is 86. The octane number of methanol is about 110.

METHANOL

Methyl alcohol or methanol, as its also known, will produce an increase in horsepower. Due to its denser mixture, Methanol requires a air/fuel ratio of 5:1 for maximum power, while gasoline only requires a 12:1 ratio. A carburetor used for alcohol must be able to supply a much higher volume of fuel to the engine than a gas carburetor, or the engine will run lean.

Alcohol is a more temperamental fuel and requires adjustment throughout the day. It's even more temperamental in cold weather.

You can also run a mixture of gas and alcohol if you use a synthetic oil. Most gas carburetors will pump a 25 percent alcohol mixture without modification. Some words of caution: Mineral oil will not mix with alcohol. If you're using an alcohol based fuel, you must use a synthetic or castor based oil. Synthetic oils blend with either gasoline or alcohol, but synthetic oils will not blend with ordinary petroleum based oils. You should always use a leading brand of 2-cycle oil. The most widely used oils are; Klotz Special Formula, a synthetic, Blendzoil, which is a castor, and Yamaha Lube.

FUEL/AIR MIXTURE

Fuel/air ratios are usually referred to as being "rich" or "lean". A rich mixture is one that has a comparatively small volume of air. A lean mixture has a comparatively large volume of air in relation to the fuel volume.

Lean mixtures are "dangerous" because they burn more slowly and require a longer time to conduct heat from the combustion chamber, plugs, cylinder walls, and piston crowns. This can lead to detonation and preignition.

The proper fuel/oil mixture is very important in a 2-cycle engine. The oil in the fuel mixture provides the only lubrication the engines moving parts receive. Excessive oil, or the improper type of oil, can cause plug fouling and excessive carbon build up. Insufficient amounts of oil can result in internal damage to the engine. Mix the fuel and oil according to the engine manufacturer's instructions. If none are available, mix the fuel with a ratio of 16 parts of gasoline to 1 part oil. 1 quart of oil with 4 gallons of gas or alcohol. This is a good ratio for normal racing conditions. Use only clean containers for measuring, and strain the mixture before pouring it into your gas tank.

Do not store fuel cans on a dirt or cement floor for any long period of time. Moisture will condense in the container making the fuel worthless.

There are several manufacturers making premixed fuels. They contain power additives and coolants blended with the fuel to increase horsepower. Premixes are available with alcohol base or a gasoline base. Insure that your selection is legal in the class you which to participate in.

Alcohol, methanol, nitro-methane and other exotic zip type additives are quite corrosive when in contact with aluminum. If you use them in your fuel, you should flush the engine with a gasoline/oil mix after each use. The most common method of doingthis, is to carry a gallon can of gas and oil, mixed with no additives, along with you. Then after the last race, remove the fuel line from the carburetor, attach a spare piece of fuel line to the carburetor and stick the open end into your can of gas and oil. Now start up the engine and run it for a few minutes. Care should be taken so as not to run the engine out of fuel. You will need to choke the carburetor until the engine pumps the fuel line full.

Be sure you have the proper carburetor for the fuel you are using.

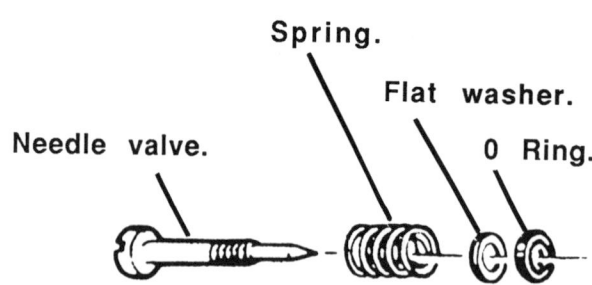

Insure that the fuel mixture needle hardware is installed correctly. Install the "O" ring first, then the washer, followed by the spring. The washer prevents the spring from cutting into the "O" ring. On a Briggs Pulsa-jet carburetor you can crimp a nickle in the slot. This will enable you to adjust the carb. without looking at it.

EXHAUST SYSTEM PREPARATION

The principle function of the exhaust system is to remove the spent exhaust gases from the engine. In the 2-cycle engine the system is designed so that a part of the gases are returned to the exhaust port at the proper time to achieve maximum power output from the engine.

4-cycle exhaust systems are much simpler than 2-cycle systems. Simple as they are much development work and hours of practice may be necessary to find the pipe that will work best for you. There is a very informative chapter on 4-cycle pipes in our book 4-Cycle Kart Engines. If you are going 4-cycle racing you should buy it. It's money well spent.

The major components of the exhaust system are the exhaust header, flex pipe on 2-cycle engines, and the exhaust pipe itself.

Proper preparation of the exhaust header is important. Few karters realize the improvement that can be gained for such a small amount of work. Of the joints in the exhaust system, the most important is the junction of the header to the cylinder block. The exhaust gas is at its highest velocity and temperature at this point, thus the transition from the cylinder port to exhaust header must be as smooth as possible. Inspect the header mounting flange. It should be flat and smooth across its entire surface, or it will not seal properly. You should always use a gasket to prevent air leaks. The gasket MUST NOT for any reason, protrude into the air stream it will disrupt the flow of gages.

The first step is to put the gasket up to the exhaust port of the engine and make sure it doesn't overlap the port. If it does, file or cut the gasket until there is no obstruction. It may also be necessary to trim the outer edges of the gasket. If you try to force an oversize gasket into place, it will have a tendency to obstruct part of the port area. Be sure to thoroughly clean both gasket surfaces of any residual gasket material.

The next step is to determine if the header overlaps the exhaust port. With the cylinder head removed. Mount the header on the engine without a gasket. Sight through the cylinder, out the port and see if here is any obstruction. If there is take a small pointed scribe and from the inside of the cylinder, scribe a outline of the exhaust port on the header flange wherever the flange overlaps the port. As a alternative, you can take a carefully fitted gasket and place it against the header. You will probably find that the header obstructs part of the port. It will now be necessary to file the header until it matches the gasket. If the amount of material to be removed is considerable, You can take it to a local kart shop. The kart shop can either mill it out, or have it done for you, for only a few dollars. I think you'll find that it's money well spent.

FLEX PIPE

On 2-cycle engines the expansion chamber is connected to the exhaust header by means of a piece of flex pipe. The flex pipe is just what it sounds like, a small piece of flexible tubing used as a connecting link between the header and the chamber. The flex must be of the correct outside diameter to prevent it from sliding up into the expansion chamber. Most chambers will accept a 1 3/4 O.D. flex. The operating characteristics of the exhaust chamber and in turn the performance of the engine can be changed by varying the length of the flex. This is more fully explained in the section on expansion chambers. New pipes are supplied with specification sheets telling you the recommended length of the total system. These lengths are usually determined by dyno testing and should, for the most part, be followed. The measurement is usually determined for good low and mid-range power. A general rule is, a short piece of flex will help the high end performance of the engine while a long piece of flex will help low end performance.

If you bought a used pipe, or it came with the kart, you will just have to experiment a little to determine which flex length is best for the track you'll be running. You may wish to make up several pieces of various lengths, so you can change pipe lengths depending upon your gearing and clutch settings. Cut the flex lengths in 1/2 inch increments.

EXHAUST PIPE

Exhaust pipe development has leveled off in the last few years. Hopefully the need to buy a new pipe every year is gone.

Dyno testing has become a major tool in producing pipes. What wins consistently this year may not win regularly next year. For the beginning karter, any of the newer models should be adequate. Forget the pipe of the year club, and concentrate on getting maximum performance from the pipe you have.

If you're buying a new pipe, buy the latest pipe on the market that's winning. By buying a new pipe, you should have one that will give you good performance for several years, unless you elect to go for a national championship.

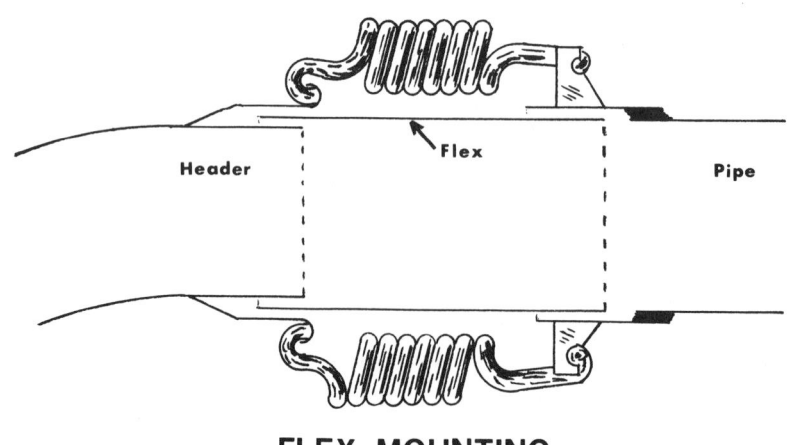

FLEX MOUNTING

It's difficult to know what you're getting when buying a used pipe. Try and get a relatively new one that was popular within the last year or two. Usually a five or ten dollar special is just that, and hardly worth the effort. There is a difference between a pipe designed for a 100 cc engine, and one designed for a 135cc engine. This is especially true of many older pipes. Normally a 135cc pipe will have a larger inlet. When buying, get one that matches the engine you are running.

EXHAUST SYSTEM INSTALLATION

Proper installation of the exhaust header is important. A loose exhaust header can cause oil to be sprayed on the rear tire and cause the kart to become uncontrollable. It will also cause the engine temperature to rise and, if uncorrected, will cause the engine to seize.

Torque the header mounting bolts to their proper value as recommended by the manufacturer. Use lock washers or Locktite. Grab the header, and be sure that it's tight. If the bolts bottom out in the cylinder the bolt will appear tight but the header may still be lose.

Yamaha exhaust headers are available in straight and 10 degree angle. From an engineering stand point the header should be mounted so the flow of gases is downward. This will conform with the taper of the exhaust port. Having said that, I have ran the header pointed up an noticed no loss of performance. The only problem with pointing it down is that it makess the camber very low and difficult to mount.

The chamber should be connected to the header with at least two springs. The springs will allow the chamber, flex, and header to vibrate without breaking. You can buy a door spring and cut it into several springs of various lengths.

The exhaust system is normally mounted to the kart in one of two ways. Some pipes have a mounting hole through the center of the chamber. If you use this type, it is highly recommended that the pipe mounting bolt contain at least one spring. This will allow the chamber to absorb road shock and vibrations without breaking the pipe or the header. The bolt should be secured with a cotter key, or double nutted. It may not keep the chamber from coming loose, but it will at least keep it from falling off the kart. Another method of mounting the exhaust system which is becoming quite popular is the cradle mount. A cradle is attached to the kart and the pipe lays in the cradle. The pipe is held in place by one or two springs or hose clamps, which wrap around the chamber.

The mounting arrangement should have some give in the system. If the system is too rigid, the stresses and vibration of racing will cause the header to crack. If possible you should keep the pipe within the rear bumper, so that an over eager competitor can't knock the pipe loose. At every race it seems that somebody retires due to something in the exhaust system coming loose or falling off. Be sure that it is not you

If your exhaust pipe has exhaust louvers, check them periodically. They should be clear so that the exhaust gases can escape. If they're gummed up or partially blocked, clean them.

Some headers have a strap for additional support. Secure the strap to a head bolt. If you are running a long pipe on a 4-cycle this must be done or the pipe will crack at the flange. Most pipes are heavy on the end and the vibration will cause them to crack. If you use a muffler as required by WKA and IKF it may be necessary to use two straps.

2-cycle or 4-cycle the pipe must not extend beyond the rear bumper.

2-Cycle or 4-cycle the exhaust must not extend beyond the rear bumber.

This pipe has a muffler and a locking coller. That's a lot of additional weight. It also has two straps.

Note: the springs streched a round the pipe for additional support

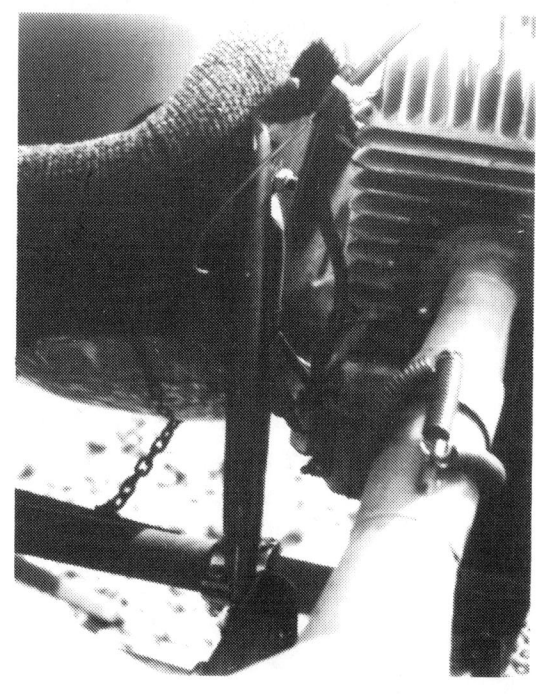

This pipe is mounted with a straight exhaust header. Note the exhaust hole is not blocked by the mounting straps.

PREPARING THE BRAKING SYSTEM

The principle function of the braking system is to slow the kart so you can negotiate a turn safely, and to stop the kart safely in an emergency. Consistently low lap times depend as much on braking ability as they do on horsepower, driving skill, or any other factor. Every fraction of a second you can maintain power before braking cuts precious seconds from your lap times. Likewise; the brakes should not impede the forward movement of the kart. I have seen many karts with the brake pads dragging on the disc, this robs the engine of vital horsepower.

Disk brakes are used in karting. They have a very good heat dissipation quality so they are not as susceptible to fading as the drum types. Disc brakes are self-cleaning and are unaffected by dirt, water, or mud on the disc. Upon applying the brakes, the puck wipes the disc clean.

The most common type of disc brake used today is the dual caliper type. It has two pistons mounted one on each side of the disc. When pressure is applied to the brake, the pistons move out until the disc is squeezed between them.

Whether you have purchased a kart, or a new brake system, you should give the system a thorough inspection. Inspect it for proper installation and operation, don't assume just because there on the kart that everything is o.k. Bad brakes may be the reason the kart was sold.

To receive top performance from your brakes you most maintain them propely. The following information will apply whether you have Enginetic, Martin Custom Products (MCP), or another brand of brake system.

Inspect the routing of the brake line to insure that it doesn't come in contact with anything that could rub a hole in it. The line should be far enough away from the exhaust pipe so that it will not touch even if the pipe should become askewed because of an accident.

When replacing the brake line, never use solid steel tubing. It will fracture under the stress and vibration of racing. It's more difficult to work with, and it will not pass technical inspection at most tracks. WKA and IKF does not allow its use.

You should inspect the brake system regularly to insure that the rear axle spins freely. Do not touch the brake disc immediately after returning to the pits. The disc may be very hot. The best way to test for drag is to remove the chain and spin the wheels. They should spin freely. If the pads drag, you're losing valuable horsepower, and experiencing increased pad wear. The pads may even heat up during the race and begin to fade. If the brakes are dragging, remove the caliper and inspect the pucks and pistons. It is not necessary to disconnect the brake line to inspect them. Check the pucks for cracks or uneven wear.

New brake pads are available in several types. Generally there is soft, medium and hard material. This is further divided in Standard and Metallic pads. The standard pads are softer and require less pressure. They also wear faster. The metallic pads are harder and are used where higher, more frequent, braking action is required and temperature of operation is higher. These linings work better hot and would last longer than softer linings under these conditions. You can tell the difference by examining the linings. The hard linings contain small bits of metallic particles which are visible. Some manufactures color code their pads. This information is available in most any kart catalog.

MASTER CYLINDER

The master cylinder must be installed in a horizontal position to function properly (fill plug up). The mounting bolts should be tight but not to tight. Excessive torque can cause distortion of the bore of the cylinder which could results in brake failure. It's a good idea to drill the bolts and secure them with saftey wire or cotter keys.

The master cylinder piston is sealed by a 0 ring type seal. If the cylinder is leaking, the seal should be replaced. Overhaul kits are available for both the master cylinder and the caliper.

When rebuilding the master cylinder here are a few things to keep in mind. The pivot pin can be driven out with a 3/16 inch diameter rod. Clean all metal parts in isopropyl alcohol or equivalent. Blow off the solvent or allow time for the solvent to evaporate completely before reassembling. Solvent will harm the new rubber parts. Lubricate the 0-ring with brake fluid before installing them on the piston. When installing the piston into the cylinder, insure that all parts remain in their proper relationship to each other.

Install the roll pin with the split side of the pin facing away from the master cylinder. As a safety precaution, the roll pin should be safety wired, or secured with a cotter pin. If you use a cotter pin, put a small washer on one end of the pin and insert it thru the roll pin and then put another washer on the pin and bend open the cotter pin.

CALIPERS

The calipers must be mounted square with the rear axle to insure proper operation between the pads and the disc. The caliper may be mounted in front of or behind, the disc. It is more common to mount the calibers toward the front of the kart. When the caliper is mounted to the rear the brake lines must loop over the disc. This should be avoided. You can image what would happen if the tubing comes in contact with a hot disc during a race. If your calipers mount in the center of the axle insure that the tubing can not be pinched between the seat and the frame rails. The bleed screw should always be mounted to the top, above the brake line fittings.

Some calipers are supplied with shims of various sizes which are used to adjust for pad wear. The shims should be arranged so the wide ends and narrow ends are together. Install enough shims between the caliper halves to give approximately 1/32" space between pads and disc. Some calipers such as MCP's are adjustable by a pair of screws in the body of the calipers. When installing the calipers insure that the pad is adjusted parrallel with the disc. If is is not the pads will wear unevenly and stopping power will be reduced. The pad spacing should be adjusted for approximately .025 clearence.

The pads must not drag on the disc. You can usually detech if the pads are dragging by giving the rear wheels a spin. I usually take a .010 feeler gauge and check to insure that it will slip between the pads and disc on both sides and top to bottom.

Another cause of the brakes dragging is because the rear axle may be walking sideways under cornering. If you find the disc is always dragging against one pad all the time try pushing the rear axle from side to side. It should not move. If it does the rear axle bearings may be worn. The disc should be centered between the pads.

During the course of the season it will be necessary to change the number of spacers or adjust the pad clearence for pad wear. Brake pads are easiely replaceable and are available from most any kart dealer. Increased spacing will cause petal travel to increase. If not corrected you may exceed the stroke of the piston in the master cylinder.

BRAKE FLUID

You should use D.O.T. 5 or better brake fluid. The higher the number the higher the temperature rating of the fluid. DOT 5 is available at most automotive stores such as NAPA.

The most important thing with brake fluid is to keep it clean. Contamination with dirt, water, or petroleum products may result in brake failure.

BLEEDING THE BRAKES

Bleeding the brakes is another way of saying that you are purging the system of air. You will know that you have air in the system because the brakes will feel spongy. If you watch the brake line while stepping on the brake petal, you will be able to see the trapped air bubbles moving from the master cylinder to the caliper. It doesn't take much of a bubble to reduce the effectiveness of the brake.

The most common way to bleed the lines is a hold over from how we bleed automotive brakes. You begin by pumping up the petal. While maintaining force on the brake pedal open the bleed valve and allow the air to excape. Close the bleed valve and release the pedal. Wait 10 seconds to allow fluid to recede into the cylinder and repeat this procedure until evidence of any air escaping from the bleed valve ceases. Check the fluid level in the master cylinder frequently.

There is a better way to bleed the brakes. I call it the Baby bottle method. Fill a baby bottle 1/2 full of brake fluid. Take a short piece of 3/16" clear hose and fill it full of brake fluid. Remember the straw trick. If you fill a straw full of coke and hold

you finger over one end the coke can't run out the other end. Slip one end over the upper most bleed screw, and place the other end into the baby bottle. It sometimes help to tie wrap or wire the hose on the bleed valve. Open the bleed valve. Now slowly pump the brake petal a few times. If there is air in the system you will see the bubbles in the baby bottle. Be careful you don't pump the master cylinder dry or you will add more air to the system. Close the bleed valve and refill the master cylinder.

TIRES

Brakes don't stop your kart, they stop the wheels. The tires on the wheels in turn stop the kart. The steering wheel itself doesn't turn your kart, it aims your front wheels. The rolling tires are what actually turn the kart. The only contact between the kart and the track is the tire contact patch or the footprint of the tire. All the useable engine horsepower must be transmitted through this very small area. This same small tire patch is responsable for getting the kart stoped. Proper selection and care of your tires is important.

Tires are available in several different tread patterns and you should select the one most suited for the type of racing you will be participating in. Racing slicks are used in sprint racing on asphalt tracks because they give you maximum rubber contact with the track. Treaded and knobby tires are available for dirt tracks where the surface is less than ideal. Tires used in karting today are tubeless.

Ten years ago tire companies only had one compound. Now we enjoy a bonanza of compounds. How do you know which one is best for you? I really can't answer that. Every kart, every driver and every track is different. For the most part your choice of tires will most likely be determined by the selection available at your local kart shop, your tire budget, or where you race. The IKF and the WKA have passed new rules concerning tires, and tire compounds, to curb the rising cost of racing.

It is doubtful if the brand of tire or tire compound is critial at this stage of your career. Perhaps more important is learning how to match the tire to your kart. Air pressure, stagger and spacing are all just as important.

If you are buying new tires don't over do it on size. As a rule I feel most karters have gone too wide in this department. Indy cars and sprint cars can run extremely wide tires because they have such a good weight to horsepower ratio. On a kart we don't have any horsepower to waste.

In the stock classes you should not need a tire wider than 4.5 inches on the front, and these may be a size to big. Wider tires only cause the kart to steer harder, and offer more wind resistance. Some karters have gone to a 7.00 inch wide tire on the rear. It's true that a wider rear track will make the kart handle better, however I suppect you can make the 6.00 inch tires will work just as well.

If you are participating in the 4-cycle or restricted Yamaha classes I would recommend you use 6.00 inch tires. They will give you less weight and scrubbing on the corners. It will also allow a slightly narrower kart. Everyone is on a wider and wider kick right how but I think this will subside somewhat. A good handling narrow kart can slip through holes the wider karts can't.

If you have a new set of tires the most important step is proper breakin. Ask your dealer for his recommendation. If you can't get a satisfactory answer use this procedure.

TIRE PRESSURE

The correct tire pressure will allow the tire to make contact with the track evenly over the full width of the tire. If the tire is under inflated, the load is concentrated on the tread sides, instead of being distributed over the whole tread. The tire walls are also subjected to greater stresses, causing the internal temperature to rise, which leads to increased tire wear. As a result, the kart will feel spongy or soft, and difficult to steer. If the tire is over-inflated, the load is concentrated around the center line of the tread, causing it to wear rapidly. Due to the reduced footprint, the kart will be difficult to hold on the track and the ride will feel harsh. The tires will feel much the same as they do on a cold day before they have reached a proper operating temperature.

The key to correct tire pressure is not to over inflate them. They are not car tires. A good starting point is 20 pounds in the rear, 15 in the front.

Changing tire pressure can be used to adjust the handling of the kart. Generally a tire will stick better as the tire pressure is decreased. Do not make any decisions based only on the feel of the kart. The stopwatch is the only thing that counts. Be sure you give the tires sufficient time to heat up before making your timed runs. I'm sure you've heard that you should only read the tire pressure then the tires are cold. That's a good idea but I've always found that the only time my tires are really cold is when I first arrive at the track. The next time you're ready to read the pressure may be a half hour after practice, or fifteen minutes, it may even be as much as two hours between your last practice and the first race. What you end up with is a lot of numbers which really don't mean a lot. I recommend you read you air pressure when you come off the track. Give yourself some time, say five or ten minutes to get through the scale and back to the pits. If you always read the pressure five minutes after coming off the track you will have some numbers that mean something.

Stagger is the difference between the circumference of the tires. This is a big car development and should be used with caution in karting. On a short oval, stagger will help steer the kart into the corners increasing your cornering speed. It will also make the kart want to steer left on the straights, so more is not always better. Stagger works because we use a locked or solid rear axle. If the left rear wheel is smaller than the right the kart will turn to the left easier than to the right.

If you are racing on a road racing type track you will want very little or no stagger. If the track should have only one right hand turn you may beable to use a little. I would recommend you not use more that 1/4 stagger until you become familiar with the handling of your kart.

Stagger is controlled by picking through the tires when you buy them, varing the air pressure, or by the amount of wear you have on them.

You should not mix brands of tires from one side of the kart to the other. The reason is because a difference in tire compound will cause them to wear at different rates.

When it becomes necessary to replace a rear tire, it is best to replace both tires at the same

This is a good example of how the brakes should be installed. The bleed valves are mounted above the brake line. The lines are short and direct. No unnecessary loops. The lines are tie wrapped to the top of frame to prevent them dragging on the ground.

time, and keep the good one for a spare if it has sufficient tread. Measure its circumference and mark it on the side of the tire. You can then save it until you have another tire of similiar size. Excessive stagger will make the kart difficult to control when changing from acceleration to deceleration, or vice-versa.

When installing a new tire you may have difficulty getting the bead to seat properly. A simple cure is to use ordinary dish soap, Smear the soap around the bead of the tire and the lip of the rim. This will help the tire slip smoothly into place.

The key to getting good wear with a soft compound tire is to drive the kart around the corners and not slide. If you are the type of karter who likes to slide around the corners, the softer compound tire will wear very fast.

Tire softers have become popular in the last few years. Tires tend to become harder as they age. Generally the tires should be painted with the softer during the week before the race, however I have seen karters painting their tires between races. If you are running a hard compound tire painting the tire may make it a little more plyable for the first couple of laps. It will also change the handling characteristics of the kart during this time. Tire softers would have to be classified as one of those non-essential items.

Some brands of tires are marked as to the direction of rotation. They should be mounted correctly, running them backwards will lead to rapid tire wear.

WHEELS

The most common type of wheels are the aluminum alloy type. Most wheels used today are of the split rim design which makes for easier mounting.

Several manufactures are now makeing a single piece wheel. This type wheel is becoming very popular because of its light weight and it's very sleet appearance. Being one piece it is not as likely to leak air, however it is more difficult to mount the tires.

The lever arm on most master cylinders have two or more mounting holes. The top hole will give you more petal travel and more leverage. The bottom hole will result in a shorter stroke and require more pressure.

49

Aluminum rims are subject to damage from an accident. The rim is easily bent and can cut the tire, if not corrected. Inspect the wheels regularly, especially after any mishaps on the track.

The front wheels can be balanced relatively easy. This may not be the professional way, but it will cure most vibration problems. Remove the front wheel and remove any excess grease from the wheel, and tighten the wheel nut only finger tight. Now slowly spin the wheel. If the wheel is out of balance, the heavy point will always stop at the bottom. You can buy small self-adhering weights at most any discount department store in the automotive department. Stick a 1/2 oz piece directly opposite the heavy end. Spin the tire again and keep repeating this process until the wheel stops at a different place each time. If three weights are required in the same area, it is possible to spread the two outside weights apart, and eliminate the third weight. When the wheel is balanced to your liking it's a good idea to lay a bead of RTV, or similar material, around the added weights, to better secure them. The RTV can be easily cut away if the wheel needs rebalanced in the future. Be sure to remove the wheel and regrease the bearings when you're finished balancing the wheels. By all means replace the wheel nut and the cotter key.

The rear tires should be balanced with a bubble balancer. There are commercially available balancers on the market.

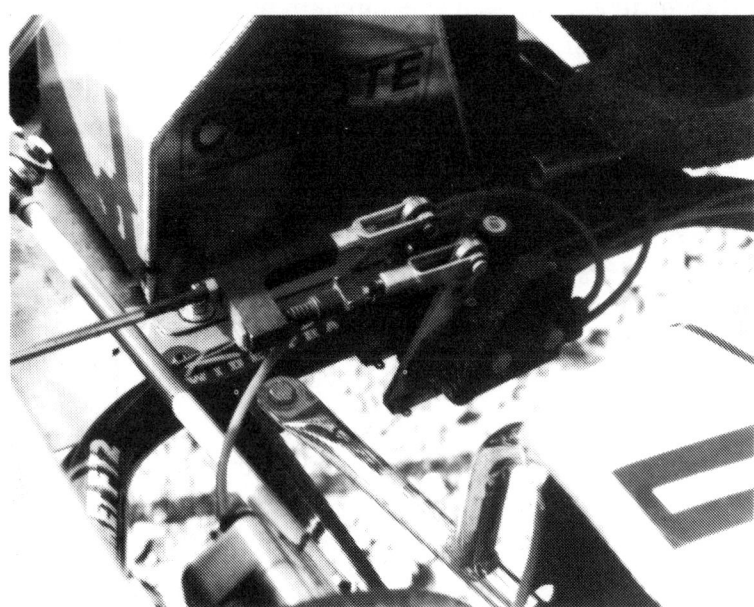

Front wheel brakes are showing up on more and more karts. They have dual master cylinders. One for the rear brakes and one for the fronts. Most four wheel brakes have a bias control on the master cylinders. The control should be adjusted so the rear brakes are applied before the front. In most classes of sprint karting four wheel brakes are not necessary.

KART PREPARATION

Proper kart assembly is vital if your karting career is to be a successful endeavor. This chapter contains recommended procedures for preparing a complete kart for a racing season. Detailed information about individual parts, such as the engine, clutch, brakes, and the exhaust system, will be found in preceding chapters. Most of the information presented will apply to either a new or used kart. Living in a northern state, I find that the winter months provide an ideal time to tear everything down for a real thorough inspection and rebuild for the coming season. There is no reason to ever go to a race until the kart and the engine is ready, "you've got to be able to finish, before you can win".

In any given race it's quite likely that as many as one third of the karts which start will not finish the race for one reason or another. Therefore any kart that is prepared well enough to last for the length of the race, has already beaten at least one third of the field before the race has even started. Another advantage of being properly prepared, is that while others are preparing their karts in the pits, you can be making use of valuable practice time. One important lesson to learn, is that problems do not go away when you ignore them, they only get worse. The best prevention is proper preparation

There are several things you can do to prevent trouble at the track. One of the first things I recommend, is that you buy a notebook and use it. It can save you a lot of headaches. When disassembling anything, remember that you are the one who's going to have to reassemble it. If theres any doubt as to what goes up or down, in or out, write it down, or scratch out a simple sketch. It only takes a minute to jot it down, and then it will be a permanent record anytime you need it, whether it's today, tomorrow, or a year from now. If you don't feel you can get it back together properly, you should wait until you're more experienced before tearing it apart, especially if the "it" is the engine.

STEERING ASSEMBLY

The steering components should be checked to insure they are tight. Also check the steering wheel to see if it's properly attached to the splined hub. The bolts must be safety wired. The hub is attached to the steering shaft with a hex nut, which must be secured with a cotter pin. On some of the older karts the splined shaft will wear, and you will not be able to tighten the steering wheel tight with the hex nut. It will be necessary in this case to replace the shaft, or fit a washer between the wheel and the nut. The washer must not tighten down on the spline of the shaft or it will not tighten the steering wheel.

The end play (up and down movement) of the steering shaft should also be checked. The bearings should be removed and inspected for wear. Some karts use a bushing, and some use a ball bearing, in either case it should be cleaned and a light coat of general purpose grease applied. If the steering shaft is mounted with locking collars they should be positioned so that there is little up and down movement in the shaft when you push or pull on the steering wheel.

It's usually a good idea to take a hold of the front wheel and see if the spindle wobbles. Excessive wobbling can be caused by two things. Worn spindle bushings or worn king-pin bolts. If they show signs of excessive wear they should be replaced.

When replacing the king-pin bolt, it should be coated with a light coat of grease. Do not over tighten the king-pin bolt nut, or you will cause the spindle bracket to bend and bind the spindle. The spindle bolt must be cotter pinned.

Inspect the steering arms to see that they are not bent. Check to see that they do not bind up when the wheels are turned in either direction. I've always found it takes a bit of work to get free travel from lock to lock, but it makes for a better handling kart. Lock should occur when the spindle arm contacts the spindle bracket, not when the steering arms come in contact with the steering shaft. To achieve sufficient travel on some of the older karts, it may be necessary to grind away a small part of the spindle arm. It may also require placing washers on either side of the bearings.

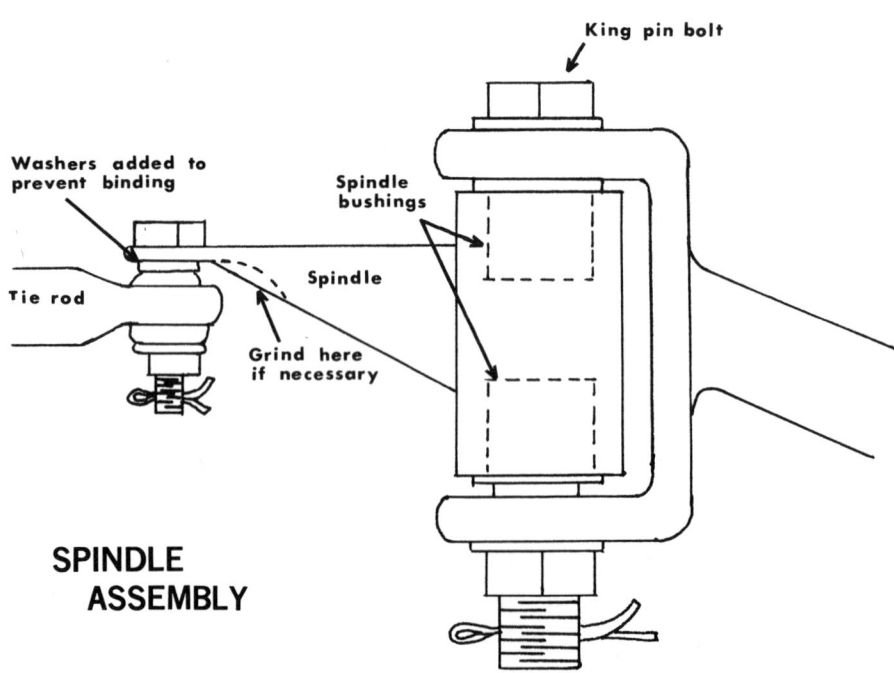

SPINDLE ASSEMBLY

Remove the front wheels and thoroughly clean the wheel bearings. Apply a light coat of wheel bearing grease to the bearing. When remounting the wheel, only tighten the wheel nut snug, not tight. The wheel should rotate freely with just a little drag, when you spin it. If the tires have a rotation arrow be sure to follow its direction.

Toe-In of the front tires should be checked. Toe-in is the effect of having the front tires pointed in slightly. This tends to offset the tendency of the wheels to spread in the front when the kart is in motion. Proper toe-in eliminates the tendency of a kart to wander at racing speeds. The recommended setting of toe-in on most karts is 1/8 inch.

Measure the distance between the front tires from center to center, at the front most point of the tires. Mark the center line with a chalk mark. Rotate the chalk mark so that it's facing the back of the kart and measure the distance center to center. The forward measurement should be 1/8 inch shorter. If this is not the case, it should be adjusted.

To adjust the toe-in remove one end of the tie-rod and adjust the tie-rod in or out, depending on which way the adjustment is needed. You should adjust both tie-rods an equal amount.

One easy method to measure toe-in is to cut two pieces of one inch wood one inch longer than the length of the tire width, and 1/2 the height. Place one on each side of the kart and measure across the front and the back of the board with a tape. The difference is the toe-in or toe-out. You can't get much simpler than that, and its easy to carry around.

REAR AXLE ASSEMBLY

Remove the rear wheels. After removing the wheels, take a piece of emery cloth and smooth the axle. Then apply a thin film of general purpose grease. The first time you have a flat tire you'll be glad you did. Check for a bent axle. You can do this with a dial indicator. A less accurate, but adequate way is to install the axle in the kart with

One of the simplest an most accurate way to measure toe-in.

the wheels removed. Position a pointed object, such as a punch or a scribe, so that it just contacts the axle out at the end. Slowly rotate the axle and observe that the axle does not rotate away from the scribe.

If a bent axle is detected, it will have to be replaced. The axle cannot be properly straightened. When ordering a new axle, remember that there are several different lengths and diameters available. American axles are in inches and European axles are in mm. Axles are also available in aluminum and steel. I refer the steel to reduce flex. Most steel axles are hollow to help reduce weight.

The rear wheels are mounted with key stock. Inspect the key stock and the axle keyways. If the key stock is worn, it should be replaced. Most of the newer axles have opposed keyways to help balance the weight.

An extra pair of locking collars can be use to prevent the axle from walking from side to side. If the axle walks it will cause a misalignment of the drive chain and it may jump off or break.

The collars must be mounted in pairs, either on the outside of the axle bearing or on the inside. This can also be done with an extra piece of key stock placed between the axle bearing and the wheel.

The key stock should be secured to the axle with hose clamps or tie wraps. Remount the wheels and tighten the wheel nuts tight. Install the cotter pins.

If the rear axle bearings have locking collars which contain set screws, check and insure that they are tight.

Check the brake disc and insure that it's not dragging on the brake pads. If it is binding up, loosen the mounting bolts on the brake caliper and determine if the brake pucks are binding the disc, or if the disc flange is causing the binding. It may be necessary to reposition the disc. If the brake pucks are worn, they should be replaced. The caliper mounting bolts should be cotter keyed. Check the fittings on the brake line at the caliper, and on the master cylinder. Use caution when tightening these fittings, they are compression fittings, and should just be tight. Check the routing of the brake line to insure that it won't drag on the track or come in contact with the brake disk, or the hot exhaust pipe. It's very difficult to be competitive without any brakes.

FUEL SYSTEM

If you are preparing a 2-cycle engine, the fuel line should be secured to the carburetor and the fuel tank with a small hose clamp, spring clip, or a couple of turns of a soft wire wrapped around the line and twisted. If the line is not sealed, the carburetor will pump air into it, and the engine will run lean and engine damage could result. It's a lot easier for the carburetor to pump air, than to pump fuel. This problem will be especially noticeable on a very hot day.

When running the fuel line between the tank and the carburetor, or between the fuel filter and the carburetor if you use one. Caution should be excerised so as not to make the fuel line to short or direct. When the carburetor demands a burst of fuel for instant acceleration the filter may momenteraly starve the fuel line for fuel. It is best to make about a 6" service loop in the fuel line to give the carburetor a reservoir to draw from.

The rear axle should be secured so the axle can't move from side to side. This can be done with locking collars or an extra piece of key stock. Be sure to secure the key stock with a tie wrap or hose clamp.

One point to remember, is that it's neccessary for the fuel tank to be vented to the outside atmosphere. Fuel cannot flow out of the tank unless air can flow in. Most tanks used in karting are vented through the fuel cap. Do not attempt to seal the cap to prevent fuel spillage. Do not try and fashion a rubber gasket that may completely seal the cap. Make sure that the vent opening is clear. If the tank is not getting air the carburetor will not be able to pump the fuel.

The fuel outlet valve in the fuel tank should be removed and the filter inspected. Not all outlet valves have filters, but if yours does, it should be cleaned occasionally. Reinstall the valve and be sure that it is tight. Some fuel tanks are equipped with twin outlets for the karters who are running twin carburetors or dual engines. The extra outlet should be plugged, and must not leak.

Some karters have elected to install an in-line fuel filter in the fuel line. I feel that this is just two more connections which can leak air. If the fuel was filtered when poured into the tank, and the fuel outlet valve has a filter, any further filtering is unnecessary. One good sign that you have an air leak in the fuel system, is bubbles in the fuel line when the engine is running. If you detect a missing in the engine, check the line for bubbles.

THROTTLE CABLE

The throttle cable is a special aircraft type, stranded cable. It is very hard, as you probably know if you've ever tried to cut it. If you solder the cable at the point you wish to cut, it will cut easier and the solder will keep the end from fraying. You can use a soldering iron or soldering gun.

The cable can be connected to the carburetor in several different ways. The spring type is very popular because it puts less side pull on the carburetor throttle shaft. The spring type may come with a set screw collar or a crimp sleeve. If you use the crimp sleeve type, be sure that the sleeve is crimped tight, so the cable cannot pull through.

The pedal end of the cable should be secured with a cable stop. Check to see that the cable moves freely within the nylon jacket.

When adjusting the cable length, you want the carburetor throttle arm to be all the way down when the throttle cable spring (located at end of the accelerator rod), is completely compressed. If the spring isn't compressed when the throttle is wide open, lengthen the cable by moving the cable stops. If the throttle doesn't open all the way when the spring is compressed, shorten the cable. When using a clevis, be careful adjusting the cable length, because if the throttle is wide open and the pedal spring is not fully compressed, any additional pressure on the pedal will pull the throttle shaft sideways, and will cause undue wear of the shaft or worse yet, cause it to snap off.

One thing to remember, is that any time you change gears or replace the chain, you may have altered the position of the engine, and you should check to insure that the cable length is still correct. You should check the throttle operation a couple of times a day to verify that the stops haven't slipped, or the cable hasn't pulled out of the clevis.

The cotter key that attaches the clevis to the throttle shaft, tends to wear, and will require changing occasionally. Check the entire cable at least once a week for frayed strands, especially at the throttle return spring, and at the brass coupling on both ends of the nylon outer cable. A throttle cable doesn't just suddenly break.

If you have trouble with the throttle not returning to the idle position the problem is most likely, the throttle return spring located on the carburetor throttle shaft. This spring breaks every so often.

MARKING

One place where many karters are negligent is in properly marking their kart. The rookie karter will most likely have to make several trips to the track before he can pick a number that's not in general use. When you do determine what number you're going to use, mark your kart, and your helmet, in large, easy to read numbers. Use black, or another dark color on white or light background. Remember, it's to your own advantage. If you want credit and recognition, timing and scoring will have to be able to distinguish who you are. The approved number panel is 7 x 10, rectangular, and is available at most kart shops for a nominal cost. The rules on number panels change from time to time. If you intend to run in sanctioned events, you should consult the current rules and regulations of the club. The color of the number panel, and the numbers are controlled by some clubs to designate classes.

WEIGHT

All IKF and WKA sanctioned races have a minimum weight limit which you'll be required to meet. The ideal situation is to be just over the limit by one or two pounds. If you are racing in stock lite, which has a weight limit of 265 and you weigh in at about 300 pounds, you may have difficulty keeping pace with the 265 pound karters. They will have a 10 per cent or greater weight advantage. 35 pounds is a lot of extra weight for a small engine. You will probably find that you will be more competitive if you add some weight and run in the stock heavy class. If you are under the desired weight, you can add just enough weight to get you over the limit. If you are going to add weight, do it in a safe manner. If you lose the weight on the track it may cause an accident. You will also be disqualified and receive no points for the race.

Weight can be added in several ways. The most common material used is lead because of its high weight per volume. You can purchase small bars of various weights, and bolt them to the frame of the kart. Be sure the weight is secure and can not fall off. Do not bolt the weight to the floor pan. The vibration of racing, and the weight of the lead, will break it in very short order. If the amount of weight to be added is small, and you have a fairly new kart, you may wish to purchase a bag of number nine shot, available were hunting supplies are sold, and pour it into both side rails. Cap the ends and lock them with a cotter key or a small bolt. The advantage of this method is that the added weight is distributed along the total length of the kart.

Lead or steel formed in a rod is also popular, and can be secured to the side rails of the kart with at least two hose clamps. Any weight added should be placed so as to equally distribute the total weight. The first should be added to the right rear to offset the weight of the driver.

FRAME TWEAKING

After an accident, you may find the kart handles differently. The kart may develop understeer, or the rear wheel may hop, even at a moderate speed. It's quite possible the frame has become slightly bent, or tweaked, as it's commonly called. The kart can also become tweaked if you only run one track year after year. You can prevent this gradual tweak from developing if about twice a year, on a Saturday or a Sunday after the racing program is completed, you run your kart ten or fifteen laps in the reverse direction.

If you suspect that the frame has become tweaked, there is one easy way to check it. You can do this by hand, but I suggest you use an inexpensive hanging weight scale. First, position the kart on a flat, level, surface with the front wheels pointed straight forward. Pick up each front wheel individually and note the weight required to lift the wheel from the ground. The weight from each wheel should be within 2 pounds of each other. If one wheel requires more effort than the other, the frame is tweaked, and should be readjusted. The simplest way to readjust it, although it may not be the most professional, is to place the heaviest front wheel up on a stand or 5 gallon fuel can. Have a friend stand on the rear wheel that is on the same side of the kart as the heaviest wheel. Now you should jump up and down, four or five times on the front wheel that was light. Put the kart back down and remeasure the front wheels. If it's still unbalanced repeat the above process again.

In some of the more advanced classes you will find that some karters tweak the frame to improve the karts handling characteristics. However, a beginner should begin with a neutral handling kart. Several of the newer karts have adjustable front spindles which can be used to adjust the handling of the kart.

KILL SWITCHES

Ignition kill switches are simple to install and convenient to use. A kill switch allows you to shut off the engine cleanly. An ignition kill switch is legal in IKF and WKA, provided that it is a single-pole, single-throw switch and connected directly to the primary winding of the ignition coil, via a single conductor wire. The switch must be grounded to the kart frame at the point of attachment. No return conductor wire from the switch to the engine is permitted. Shielded electrical cable is not allowed.

The Briggs 4-cycle engine comes with a kill switch. It is legal to use it if you wish.

ENGINE MOUNT

There are several different methods of mounting the engine to the kart. The most important thing is to be sure that the engine crankshaft is perpendicular to the rear axle. Some of the karts use a two-piece mount. One piece mounts directly onto the kart frame, while the second piece mounts on the engine. When installing the frame piece, position it so that the mounting slots for the engine are at a right angle to the rear axle. A framing square can be used to properly align the piece. Make sure the mounting bolts are tight. Most of the newer karts use a single engine mount which attaches to the frame rails with a pair of butterfly type brackets.

For the initial installation, place the engine in the center of the adjustment range and tighten it down. Take a piece of new chain and make it to the proper size. This will allow you plenty of adjustment if you need to change gears at the track, without having to make a new chain each time.

ENGINE PREPARATION

Preparing the engine for a racing season is a major undertaking. For the beginner just starting out in his first year of racing. I recommend that you have a kart shop or a more experienced karter prepare the engine for you. Everyone likes to feel that they can do their own work, but one should not feel ashamed to admit that they have limited knowledge. Veteran karters will tell you that they learn something new almost every time they race. A little knowledge is more dangerous than none at all. A kart shop can hone the cylinder and fit a new piston and rings, if necessary. They can install new seals, grind the valves, and clean up any thing else that needs attention. They will return the engine to you in good operating condition ready for another racing season.

After the engine has been returned to you from the kart shop, it will still be necessary for you to do some additional preparation. You will need to install the thermocouple for the temperature gauge if one is used. Mount the motor mount, chain guard, and clutch. As you can see, there's still plenty of work to be done before you're properly prepared for racing.

When working on an engine don't jam a screwdriver into the exhaust port to prevent the crankshaft from rotating. This can damage the piston, an/or the ports.

With the new electronic ignition systems it's no longer necessary to set the point timing. However; some engines still use points so I will cover the proper procedure for setting the points here. If you have electronic ignition you can skip this part.

POINT TIMING

Setting the engine timing requires time and patience. You should not attempt to set the timing unless you have some understanding and knowledge of the proper procedure. Setting the points with a feeler gauge is not recommended for today's high power kart engines. It should only be used if you have no other way to set them.

If you install a new breaker point assembly, it's advisable to clean the surface of the new points before the engine is run. Do not run a point file between the contacts before installing them, it will cause microscopic scratches and cause them to burn. Clean them with contact cleaner. Do not use gasoline. As a final step pull a piece of paper thru them. This will remove any remaining residue.

DEGREE WHEEL METHOD

One way to time your engine is with a degree wheel, a simple timing, or continunity, light, and a piston stop. Kits containing all the necessary items are available at most kart shops. You can make the timing light out of a flashlight by sodering two leads to it. The flashlight should light when the leads are touched together. The piston stop can be made out of an old sparkplug. Break out the insulator then drill and tap the center for a bolt.

Mount the degree wheel on the crankshaft on the side of the engine opposite the points if possible. You will need to make a pointer. Use a piece of wire. Mount it to an engine bolt near the degree wheel and bent it so it points to the markings on the wheel.

The first thing we must do is find TDC (top dead center). Remove the sparkplug and install the piston stop. Slowly turn the crankshaft either way until the piston touches the piston stop. Take a reading from the degree wheel. Turn the crankshaft in the opposite direction until the piston again stops at the piston stop. Take a second reading. One half the untraveled distance between the two stops is TDC. For an example, the untraveled distance is 62 degrees, top dead center is 31 degrees. To make "0" on the degree wheel TDC, loosen the wheel and rotate it until the pointer is pointing at 31 degrees. How turn the crankshaft in the opposite direction until the piston again stops at the piston stop. The reading should be 31 degrees. If necessary repeat this until the reading is the same at both stops. When that is true "0" is top dead center. You can now remove the piston stop.

Disconnect the breaker point lead from the coil. Connect one lead from the timing light to the breaker point lead and the other lead to the engine.

Slowly rotate the crankshaft in the direction it runs, watching the timing light. When the points close the timing light should be on, slowly continue rotating until the timing light goes out. This is the place the points will fire the sparkplug. Read the degree wheel. If the reading is 23, then the timing is 23 degrees before TDC. If the desired reading is 21 degrees, readjust the points and repeat the test until the desired reading is obtained. Repeat the test after everything is tighten down to insure nothing as changed.

DIAL INDICATOR METHOD

A more accurate way of setting ignition timing can be accomplished with a dial indicator and a timing light. If you have a depth gauge, it can be used in place of a dial indicator. With a dial indicator, it's possible to determine the exact location of the piston at the precise instant that ignition occurs.Remove the spark plug. Install the dial indicator on the cylinder head. Disconnect the point wire and connect the timing light between the point wire and a ground, like the cylinder head.

Rotate the crankshaft until the piston is at top dead center. The pointer of the indicator will change direction when the piston reaches TDC. Now set the pointer on the dial indicator to zero.

Rotate the crankshaft in the direction the engine runs until the timing light goes off. Note the reading on the dial indicator This is the position of the piston in inches before TDC. The factory recommended setting is, 26 degrees, this translates into .110 inches in a stock engine. To be exact this must be computed for each engine.

Adjust the points until the proper reading is obtained. Retighten the breaker point mounting screw before taking the measurement. It will affect the point setting. It's usually a good idea to spin the engine over a couple of times, and then verify the timing.

IGNITION COIL LAMINATION GAP

The following procedure should be followed to set the ignition coil lamination gap.

Turn the flywheel so that the magnets are at the bottom most position. Loosen the two mounting screws. Pull up on the coil and tighten the mounting screws. Rotate the flywheel so the magnets are at the top most position, directly under the legs of the coil.

Place a 0.012 feeler gauge between the coil legs and the flywheel magnets. Loosen the two coil mounting screws and the magnets will pull the coil down. Push down on the coil and tighten the mounting bolts.

Rotate the flywheel to remove the feeler gauge. Rotate the flywheel to verify that it has proper clearance. There should be no contact with the coil. The 0.012 setting is a tuning aid. The timing of the engine can be changed slightly by increasing or decreasing this gap.

REED VALVE ENGINES

The reeds vibrate very fast at high RPM. Anything sucked up by the carburetor passes through the reeds, and it doesn't take much to chip one. They're cheap enough to replace, and it only takes a few minutes. It's usually a good idea to carry along an extra reed block already made up. Before installing the reed block assembly, slightly bend the reed stops until they just touch the manifold when reinstalling it into the engine. This will enable the reeds to open as far as possible.

Before installation of the carburetor take the gasket that fits between the carburetor and the engine, and insure that it does not protrude into the path of the fuel flow. Trim the inside edges as necessary. Now mount the carburetor. Use lock washers and be sure that the nuts are tight.

AIR FILTERS

The advent of the side-mounted engine has moved the carburetor throat in line with the front tire, making it susceptible to sucking up stones, dirt, rubber, and other debris kicked up by the front tire. The best solution to this problem is one of the new foam filters. The filter comes with an adapter which mounts on the front of the carburetor. The foam filter then mounts to the adapter with a single large clamp, so that it can be easily removed for cleaning. The filter can be cleaned by soaking in solvent. Allow the filter to thoroughly dry before using. If you do not wish to use a filter, you should at least use some type of stone shield or guard. In dirt track racing it's not uncommon to see plastic jugs modified for use as dirt shields.

WKA now requires an approved air box on Yamaha engines. The air box is required to reduce the intake noise level of 2-cycle engines.

In 4-cycle racing any filter is allowed but the adapter must conform to the tech manual. The tapered edge must not be radius more than .250". If you mount the adapter you must use a filter.

THERMOCOUPLE

To install the thermocouple washer remove the spark plug from the engine. Then remove the standard washer from the plug. Install the thermocouple washer on the plug and reinstall the plug in the engine. Be sure that the thermocouple washer is properly seated in the head. It must fit flat on the head. If the thermocouple washer is very thick it may be necessary to use a longer reach spark plug. Tighten the spark plug and torque it.

Route of the thermocouple cable so it cannot come in contact with the clutch or chain. Leave a service loop so the cable is not drawn tight by engine vibration.

CHAIN GUARD

A chain guard is required. There are many different types on the market. You can even make your own if you wish. Insure that it will not interfere with the proper operation of the chain. The purpose of the chain guard is to prevent injury in case the chain breaks.

Personal Expense Report

ENTRY FEES			PARTS			
DATE	TRACK	AMOUNT	DATE	PAID TO	FOR	AMOUNT
	TOTAL				TOTAL	

TRAVEL EXPENSES				
NUMBER OF TRIPS	MILES	TRACK	MPG OR EST COST p/TRIP	
				ENTRY FEES _____
				PARTS _____
				TRAVEL _____
				MISCELLANEOUS _____
				SEASON TOTAL _____

ACCESSORIES

This chapter covers some of the many accessories which are available such as; temperature gauges, starters, stopwatches, tools, and supplies. The section on temperature gauges deals with the need for a gauge and a brief description of the major brands on the market. This chapter also covers the most important part of any starting system, the battery.

I do not recommend you buy everything that is presented in this chapter, but you should be aware of what is available.

TEMPERATURE GAUGES

Temperature gauges are becoming more and more popular, A temperature gauge is expensive, but in the long run it can save you many dollars worth of repair costs.

Temperature gauges have evoled into many different styles. Large digit, small digit, lighted, nonlighted, some with memory and what have you.

Basically there is two temperatures that are of concern in karting. Cylinder head temperature and exhaust temperature.

The digital type has a LCD (Liquid Crystal Display) readout. The unit itself has no moving parts. Digatron is the leading manufacturer of digital meters for karting.

If you are running a 2-cycle engine, I fully recommend that you use some type of cylinder head temperature gauge. A temperature gauge can be beneficial on a 4-cycle engine but is not necessary. A temperature gauge is also not necessary if you are running a stock Yamaha, but if you are running a modified engine you should use one. It's very difficult to go racing without "tweaking" around on the carburetor, and there is no better way to tell whats going on inside the engine, than to monitor the head temperature. The number one cause of engine failure is piston seizure, or as its more commonly known "sticking it". The most common cause of piston seizure is high speed running with a lean fuel mixture. This is caused by the high speed needle on the carburetor being set too lean. This reduces the fuel to air ratio, and robs the engine of much needed lubrication when it's most needed, When the piston over heats it grows in size until the piston to cylinder clearance is reduced to zero, causing the piston to stop or stick. Fortunately, piston seizure is preceded by a sharp rise in cylinder head temperature. In most cases, there is time to open up the high speed needle, or to at least choke the carburetor with your hand thus forcing it to pump more fuel until you have time to readjust the carburetor.

DIGITAL GAUGES

The Digatron temperature gauge is a digital readout meter. The unit mounts in the center of the steering wheel. This type meter has a liquid crystal display (LCD).

The gauge continuously monitors the engine head temperature. The sensor mounts under the spark plug in place of the standard washer.

The Digatron is powered by nine volt batteries. The unit has an on/off switch, so that the unit can be turned off whenever you're not on the track. This helps to prolong battery life. The newer meters have automatic shut off. The meter automatically reads its battery condition so you have some warning when the battery is getting low.

The Digatron gauge is also available with a tachometer function to monitor the RPM of the engine. The sensor for the tachometer is connected to the spark plug wire.

This is a valuable asset for selecting the proper gear ratio. It's also used to set the clutch engagement point

STARTERS

The most common type of starter has become the hand held starter similar to the type used at Indy. This type starter starts the engine from a nut located on the clutch side of the engine. The biggest disadvantage to the hand held starter is probably cost. The hand held models usually use a light weight starter, manufactured by Lucas, or one of the small minicrank starters. The starter is then mounted to a pair of handles. Adding bicycle hand grips will make the starter easier to handle. The starter switch and solenoid is mounted next to one of the handles. The starter shaft should be equipped with a one-way ratchet drive that will allow the starter to disengage when the engine starts. Most karters transport the battery and starter in some type of kart, wagon or carrier.

When connecting the wires from the battery to the starter, heavy gauge wire is required. Connect the plus (+) lead to the solenoid and the negative (-) lead to the starter body. After you have connected the wires, take the starter and touch the handle to the negative terminal of the battery, the starter should not run. If it does, reverse the wires to the starter or the battery. If you don't the starter may be left running accidentally. This will run down the battery or worse yet, burn out the starter. Any exposed terminals should be protected to prevent any possible shorts.

The most important part of any starter system is the battery. If you don't have a good battery and keep it charged, you're just asking for trouble. Buy a battery big enough to do the job. A compact car battery will not be able to stand up to the constant charging and discharging you will require of it. When buying a new battery, the thing to look for is the "amp hour" rating. Most batteries are marked with a amp hour rating, or a watt rating. To determine amp hours from watts, simply divide the watts by the volts which is 12. 3000 watts divided by 12 volts equal 250 amp hours. In this case, the higher the amp hours the better. A battery with 400 amps is good, 600 amps is better.

Caution should be exercised when moving or charging a battery, to avoid spilling or splashing. Batteries contains a liquid composed of sulfuric acid and water. If the battery acid is splashed on clothing, it will eat a hole in it. The acid can be neutralized by flushing the area, first, with a solu-

The hand held starter has become standard. Just like at Indy. This one even has wheels, which is really nice when the race is red flagged and you have to start the kart on the track.

tion of 1/2 baking soda, 1/2 water, and then flushing it again with clean water. The battery should only be charged in a open, well ventilated area. An explosive gas mixture forms in each cell when the battery is being charged. Keep the battery clear of a spark or open flame, because the flame can ignite the gas, causing an explosion.

STOPWATCH

A stopwatch is a must for any serious karter. There is just no way to tell how fast you're going, or the effects of a change you've made, unless you use a watch.

A stopwatch is also valuable when visiting a new track. It will allow you to clock the competition and determine what is an acceptable time. This way you can determine if you have your kart properly prepared to be competitive.

There are two types of stopwatches on the market. The more common mechanical watches, and the newer digital models. The mechanical watches have been around for a long time, and comes in several types and prices. You don't need a $50.00 watch to do the job, when a $20.00 watch is more than adequate. The most common type used in karting is a 1/10 second with a 30 second sweep. It allows you to read the time in hundredths, with some degree of accuracy. The important thing is to get one that is easy to read and use.

The biggest disadvantage of the mechancal watch is that you can only time every other lap, unless you buy two watches and a holder, that will allow you to start one and stop the other simultaneously.

The new digital watches are a major improvement in stopwatches, however digital types are more expensive than the mechanical type. Their greatest advantage is that, if you buy the right kind, you can time every lap. It's a real time saver when setting up a clutch, or when there's limited practice time.

The two most popular brands are the Accusplit, and the Cronus. They have an easy-to-read digital display which provides instant error free readouts. They are visible in any light, and display two decimal points, (hundreds of a second) with greater accuracy than the mechanical watches. They have no moving parts and are virtually trouble free, if not abused.

The only disadvantage of the digital, if it has one, is that it operates from a battery. The best thing to do is change the battery once a year, whether it tests bad or not. It's recommended that you carry a spare along, just in case.

Mechanical or digital, the watch should be handled with care. It's a precision instrument and should be treated as such. Whichever stopwatch you use, keep in mind, it's only as accurate as the person operating it. Always use a stationary object, such as the starting line, tree, or a light pole, to time from. Always use the same object every lap. Always push the button the same way. Some of the mechanical watches may have some slack or play, in the button. You can take this play out without tripping the button. It will allow you to get a more accurate reading.

Several of the new digital watches offer many features which are not really necessary for karting. Dual event and split time, just are not used under normal conditions. If you can find a digital without these features, you should be able to get a good price. Cronus has recently reduced the price on their single event timer to the point where its cheaper than some of the more expensive mechanical watches.

Discount stores are being flooded with cheap ditial stopwatches. Make sure the watch will do what you want it to do. Try the watch before you buy to insure you can time consecutive laps, not cumulative time.

SPARE PARTS

The question of what spare parts do you need to carry along with you each week has only one real answer. That is, carry one of everything. To spend a countless number of hours in preparation, maybe an hour or more in driving time to get to the track, and then not beable to compete because of the failure of a two or three dollar part, is not only discouraging, but a waste of your valuable time.

The most common parts to fail are the spark plug and the chain. You should have at least two new plugs with the gap already set, so that if need be, you can change it on the starting grid quickly.

Next on the list of most often lost or broken parts is in the exhaust system. It's a good idea to have a couple of exhaust gaskets, as well as an extra set of header mounting hardware. Also carry a selection of extra springs for the flex pipe if you use one.

Some other items which may occasionally need to be replaced, are the following; you should carry an extra high-speed and low-speed needle. Be sure to include the associated hardware, spring, flat washer, and rubber O-ring. On a Briggs engine you should have an extra carburetor and fuel tank. They break often. Don't forget extra mounting screws.

If you run a reed valve engine carry an extra pair of reeds. In fact, it's even better if you have a complete reed block, since this will make replacement quicker.

You should have an extra axle nut or spring clip for the front and back, if they're not the same. It is also a good idea to have an extra length of fuel line and brake line already made up. Other items to have would be an extra throttle cable, and extra set of brake pucks, and an extra nut for the engine crankshaft, both flywheel and clutch side. 2-cycle karters should carry a extra clutch/starter nut, As you can see, there is no end to the list. In reality, the list depends on how well prepared you are before you leave for the track.

Other important items you should consider would be a tire pump and a good quality air pressure gauge. A roll of soft wire, and a roll of good quality tape, are also useful items. Don't forget the fuel cans and a extra quart of oil. Generally, fuel and oil is available at most tracks. In addition, take along extra clutch oil and brake fluid.

One of the most useful things I've found to carry is a coffee can or cigar box full of miscellaneous nuts and bolts. A good assortment of cotter keys is also handy to have along. A can of waterless hand soap and some rags are a must. If you mix your own fuel be sure to take along a measuring cup in case you need to mix some additional fuel at the track. It's also a good idea to have an extra chain of the proper length made up.

The list just grows and grows, however, it is always best to play it safe and take as much as you can. If you need something at the track you forgot, don't hesitate to ask your fellow karters. After you've been around awhile, you will find that most karters are helpful and they'll let you borrow most anything you need to get running. Remember though it works both ways. If you can help someone else, do it. You'll soon find out that they'll be more eager to assist you when you need it, if you are also ready to help a fellow karter. It's cheap insurance.

I won't go into a long discussion on tools, since anyone going into karting should have a good working knowledge of hand tools, what they are, and how to use them. A good tool box is of paramount importance. I will only mention some of the special purpose tools that you may find it necessary to purchase.

One of the most important tools you will need to buy is a torque wrench. When buying a new one, you should get one that reads in inch-pounds.

4-cycle people should carry the special hobbed tooth flywheel wrench for easy removal of the flywheel or clutch nut.

There are several different types of clutch and flywheel pullers on the market. You will need one if you intend to remove either. The taper of the shaft retains the hub or flywheel, even after the nut has been removed. Do not remove the flywheel with a pry bar and a hammer. You are working on a racing engine, not a lawn mower.

Keep in mind that the US is switching to the metric system. To the karter, that means that standard wrenches won't fit metric nuts, and vice-versa. If you have a metric engine, you will need to buy the necessary metric tools to maintain it. All the foreign engines are metric engines. It's a shame that we need to purchase two sets of tools, but unfortunately nothing can be done about it. One piece of test equipment which I find very helpful is a Volt-Ohm Meter, or as its sometimes called, a VOM. The VOM is a meter that can read both AC and DC voltage as well as ohms. The ohm is a measurement of resistance. The VOM can be used to check the Magneto coil. It can also be used to check for proper operation of the points (if you engine has them) while troubleshooting the engine. Small pocket-size VOM's are available, ranging in price from 15 to 20 dollars, at most electronic supply houses such as Radio Shack.

SOFT TOOLS

I always carry a tube of RTV adhesive sealant in my tool box. RTV is made by several manufacturers, and the brand you buy is not important. RTV is a general purpose one part silicone rubber, sealant. It is available in either white or clear. It has a thick consistency and will not flow under its own weight. It can be worked into cracks and holes. The area to be repaired should be clean as possible. Use solvent to clean it. RTV dries to a semi-resilient consistency so it is always pliable and resistant to vibration. It can be peeled off by hand, if need be. Also it can be used to repair a damaged fuel tank and to secure wheel weights to the wheels. In addition, it can be used as a gasket compound. RTV normally forms a tack-free skin within an hour. It cures to a firm silicone rubber in 24 hours.

I also carry a tube of loctite. You will find more information about loctite in the section entitled Anaerobics.

If you live in a northern state you will need to insure that soft tools such as RTV, Loctite, and paint are not allowed to freeze. During the winter months move these type things into the house or basement.

Some of the soft stuff you will want to have around. Never-Seez for those things you want to stay free, and Loctite for those you want to stay tight. Blueing which is used to check contact between mating surfaces. Don't forget RTV.

KART & ENGINE CHECK LIST

The following is a check list of items which should be checked during the practice session and after every race.

ITEMS TO BE INSPECTED

_____The chain should have 1/4 inch slack.

_____The sprocket should be tight and properly aligned.

_____Front and rear wheel nuts should be tight with cotter keys in place.

_____Motor mount hardware should be tight.

_____The carburetor should be tight.

_____The exhaust header should be tight.

_____On a 2-cycle check the flex springs.

_____The accelerator should open the throttle all the way.

_____The spark plug wire should be secure.

_____The rear axle should spin freely. Brakes not dragging.

_____Check for sufficient fuel for the next race.

TRACKSIDE

This chapter covers a multitude of items that can only be performed properly at the track. There is no substitute for practice. This chapter will tell you how to best use this valuable time. Also covered is how to select the gear that best works for you. In addition, I have attempted to explain some of the mysteries of setting up the clutch.

A detailed explanation of the correct way to drive a race course is presented. Finding the fastest line through the corners, and locating the proper brake points, are also covered.

PRACTICE

Practice is a vital time for any driver no matter how good he is. For some drivers it's a time to learn the circuit. For all drivers, it's time to become familiar with existing conditions.

One of the most important parts of practice time is devoted to learning how to drive the track. It's safe to say, the smoothest driver is the one with the most experience. You can gain a lot of insight into the art of driving just by watching the track champion. Watch how he enters and exits the turns. Between your practice sessions walk around the track and observe his line through each corner. When he brakes, and when he accelerates. If you get on the track at the same time, follow him, watch and learn his line around the track.

On most tracks, you can see the most popular line by looking at the rubber groove laid down on the track by other karters. This is especially helpful on unfamiliar tracks. Some of the older tracks will have a groove worn through the top of the asphalt. It may be rougher but time has proven that its the fastest line around the corner.

Learning the track is only part of the job of practice. It is a time to sort out the kart to make sure it is properly set up to suit the prevailing conditions, and its a time for checking gear ratios. A driver must decide whether the gain in the corners is worth the slight loss on the straights. A driver may decide to wait until after the first heat, so he has time to evaluate his performance before making a decision on which gear to use.

Practice is a time for checking clutch slippage. Should more weight be added, or some removed? Did you remember to put oil in the clutch, or check to be sure that it has oil in it.

Practice is also a time to verify that everything is tight. After making several laps, come in and give the kart and engine a good going over. Check the carburetor, the motor mounts, and the exhaust system. Check them with a wrench, don't just eyeball them. On a 4-cycle be sure to check the carburetor mounting bolts and the fuel tank bolts, they have a habit of virbrating loose. Practice is time to adjust the carburetor for existing weather conditions. If you prefer not to adjust the carburetor during the race, this will be your only time to adjust it. The settings will change throughout the day, especially if the weather changes dramatically, but you can still get a good initial setting.

During the practice session, you should pick your braking points. A corner really begins when you start to brake. You should mentally record certain landmarks so you can quickly locate the same spot on each succeeding lap. Pick a tree, fence post, or a crack in the track, or anything that is permanent. If you have time, try driving a little deeper into the corners each lap. Your lap times should keep dropping. If you have the track pretty much to yourself you can keep this up until you spin out. If you do, be careful.

During practice and the race itself you should study all of the drivers in your class. This is very important if you compete at one particular track most of the time. Some drivers don't have the brains they were born with. You will soon know who they are, give them plenty of room, they will usually take care of themselves. Don't attempt to pass them in a turn under any circumstances. They will go in and crash and take you out with them, and most likely blame you for the crash. There are other drivers who you can race with wheel-to-wheel, any place on the track. You will learn to respect them and they will respect you.

One important thing to remember is that practice and qualifying sessions are controlled by the local track owners and operators. If you're going to a new track, ask someone who's been there. If you plan to race at the same track again I recommend that you get the phone number of the track operator, so that if the weather is inclement, you can call ahead and see if they plan to race. Naturally, it's a lot cheaper to phone first than to haul your kart to the track, only to find that the race has been canceled.

Practice time at most local races is commonly called "open practice" where every one is allowed on the track at the same time. At the IKF and WKA races, the practice session is usually divided into several short sessions for each class. Take it upon yourself to find out when your practice time will be.

Almost all tracks run classes with weight limits. The scale will be located in the pit area, and you should take time before or during the practice session to verify your weight. If you've done any racing at all, you are aware that not all scales weigh the same. Most of the scales are old, weather-beaten, and have not been taken care of properly. You can almost always hear someone complain about the scales being wrong. Maybe they are right, and the scales are off, but it really doesn't matter. Everyone has to weigh on the same scale. If it's wrong for you, it's wrong for the competition also. The important thing is to make sure that you yourself make the limit.

If you come off the track light, you will be disqualified from that race, and will lose any points that you may have earned. When you weigh your kart, remember to include your helmet and jacket. Also, remember that a full tank of fuel can add five pounds to your weight. It won't be full after the race. You should take that into consideration when weighing.

It should be apparent that practice time is very valuable. You should strive to arrive at the track so as to be able to make use of as much of the allowed practice time as possible. You can always find guys spending the practice time doing tasks which should have been done before arriving at the track. Don't be one of these.

REGISTRATION

One aspect of racing where the rookie seems to do better than the veteran is in Signing-In. I don't know why people are hesitant about signing-in, as it only delays the qualifying, and makes it more difficult for the registrar. Sign in early. If for some reason you're unable to qualify for the race, most local tracks will refund your entry fee. One advantage of signing in early is that in the case of inclement weather some tracks elect to dispense with qualifying, and start the first event in the order of registration. This means that the first person to sign in starts on the pole position. Some tracks will not let you practice until you have signed in.

CARBURETOR ADJUSTMENT

Carburetor adjustment is perhaps the most critical bit of knowledge that a karter must learn. No other single adjustment has more impact on performance and reliability. A seemingly innocent twist of the high speed mixture needle can lead to almost instantaneous destruction of an engine.

On 2-cycle engines there are three major carburetor components which require accurate adjustment if the engine is to perform properly. The high-speed mixture needle, the low speed mixture needle, and the fulcrum lever.

The only way to accurately tune the carburetor, is on the track. You can not do it with the back of the kart up on blocks, or a stand. The engine must be operating under a loaded condition to be adjusted properly.

On track tuning enables an accurate adjustment, taking into consideration track conditions, weather conditions, and different fuel/oil mixtures. Adjustment of the carburetor with the rear wheels raised, means little. Don't waste your time, take it out on the track.

First, obtain an initial setting by turning both needles in a clockwise direction until they contact their seats. Do not force the needles in too tight, as this will damage the seat. Turn both needles out, counter clockwise, one and one fourth turns. This setting should normally have the engine running rich. Starting rich is best, because to lean a mixture, might seize a piston before you have time to get things adjusted.

Take the kart out on the track and run several slow laps to warm up the engine. Adjustments shouldn't be made until the engine is warm, even though the engine will probably four cycle, or blubber most of the way around the track. A 2-cycle engine is said to be 4-cycling when the cylinder is too rich causing the plug to foul. It begins to fire everyother revolution instead of every time. This condition can usually be cured by leaning out the high speed needle. After the engine is warm, lean (close, turn clockwise) the high speed needle 1/16th of a turn at a time, until the engine begins to run smoothly all the way to the end of the longest straightaway. If you have a temperature gauge, keep a eye on it, so that the engine is not over heated.

After a couple of more laps, open the high-speed needle just slightly, to richen the fuel/air mixture. If after richening just slightly, the engine starts to four cycle at the end of the straightaway, the setting is very close to correct. It is important that the entire lap be driven at racing speeds, because slow speeds will cause the crankcase to fill up with excess fuel and give a false reading on the straight. Low-speed acceleration and idle characteristics can be adjusted, using the low-speed needle. After setting the high speed needle, run a few laps at a slow speed, about the same speed traveled when lining up on the pace laps. If the engine has a tendency to load up when you first start to accelerate, the low-speed needle is set too rich. You can also glance at the exhaust. If it's smoking heavily your low-speed is too rich. Lean the low-speed needle by turning clockwise about 1/8th turn, then recheck the high-speed performance. Leaning the low-speed will also lean the high-speed needle, and it will need to be richened. After changing the high speed needle recheck the low-speed performance.

If the low-speed performance is sluggish coming out of the corners, the low speed needle is probably set too lean. Richen the low speed needle by turning it counter clockwise about 1/8th turn. Then recheck the high speed performance.

The most important thing to remember is that if you change one needle, you must recheck the other because they interact.

Carburetor adjustment should be checked throughout the day, since temperature and humidity change constantly. Be sure to properly warm up the engine before making any adjustments. If you set the carburetor while the engine is cold, it will lean out once it reaches proper operating temperature, and unless you readjust it, it will seize the piston.

Another thing that will affect the carburetor settings is the fuel/oil mixture. If you change the fuel mixture, or change types of fuel, it will be necessary to readjust the carburetor. You should get use to adjusting the carburetor with out looking at it. You can develop a feel for it. During a race you should not take your eyes off the track.

Check the idle screw setting. It should be set so that the engine is running just slightly above stall speed. If the idle speed is adjusted too high, you will have difficulty setting the low-speed needle properly because the high-speed valve will allow some fuel to pass through it. If the carburetor is adjusted properly the engine should idle smoothly.

It's hard to say at what height to set the fulcrum arm. The way I've found most successful, is to start by setting the fulcrum arm just flush with the body of the carburetor. Bolt the carburetor together and air check it with the pressure gauge used to air check the engine. Connect the air hose to the fuel inlet, and pump the pressure up to four or five pounds. If the fulcrum arm is set right, the fuel inlet will be closed, and the carburetor should hold the pressure. If the fulcrum arm is set too high, the fuel inlet needle will be open, and the carburetor will not hold air pressure. Care should be used not to pump the pressure too high, or the pressure will over come the pressure of the lever inlet spring, and open the valve, no matter what the fulcrum arm setting. The carburetor may also fail to hold air pressure if the gaskets are not seated.

From here take the kart out and try to adjust the carburetor. If you find that you have the needles turned all the way out and the engine is still starved for fuel the fulcrum arm should be bent up. If you find the needles are turned all the way in and the engine is running to rich the fulcrum arm should be bent down. If the fulcrum arm is set right for the fuel you are using the needles should be about 1 turn out when all is said and done.

In order to make it easier to adjust the carburetor you can purchase extended adjustment needles for both the high and low-speed needles, or you can have a small washer brazed on the head of the low-speed.

I recommend inspecting the spark plug after you feel that everything is set up properly. It will tell you if the carburetor setting is close. To get a good plug reading, it is necessary to run a couple of consecutive hot laps, terminating as close to the pit lane as possible. You should kill the engine upon entering the pit lane. Do not run a cool off lap, or blip the accelerator coming into the pits or you will mask the true plug reading. Do not choke the engine to shut it off, use a kill switch if you have one. If you follow these simple guidelines, the plug will give you an accurate reading of engine performance and carburetor settings.

Symptoms to watch for while adjusting the carburetor are listed below:

The adjustment is too lean if:
1. There is no exhaust smoke.
2. Engine runs better at part throttle.
3. Choking makes the engine run better.
4. The tip of the spark plug appearsgray or ash white.

The adjustment is too rich if:
1. The exhaust smoke is excessive.
2. Choking makes the engine run worse.
3. The tip of the spark plug appears wet or sooty.

Adjusting a 4-cycle carburetor is not nearly as precise an operation as a 2-cycle. If a 4-cycle carb is setup correctly it is not uncommon to make no adjustments to the needle during a race day.

On a Briggs Pulsa jet carburetor you should remember that if the needle is adjusted about two turns out it is at full flow and turning the screw out further will have no effect on fuel flow. If more fuel is required it is necessary to install a larger jet.

The guide lines for adjusting the carburetor are pretty simple. If the engine is too hot turn the screw out. If it's running cool turn the screw in. If turning the screw in doesn't help heat up the engine change the jet. If the engine misses going down the straightaway try adjusting the screw 1/2 turn each way. If this doesn't help, change the spark plug. If that doesn't help try replacing the carburetor diapham.

GEARING

It is generally difficult for the new karter to know what the proper gear is. The first thing you should do is talk to some other drivers of your class and weight. This is generally a good starting point. As a rule, most new karters have few gears to choose from, and with the rising cost of sprockets, it's not economically feasible to go out and buy all of them. So the question becomes, do you need a sprocket with more teeth, or one with less? The best way to determine the correct gear ratio for you is with a stopwatch. You just cannot tell, driving around in the kart, which gear is the fastest. A stopwatch is the only answer.

The less teeth on the gear, the more speed you will have on the straightaways, until you reach the peak horsepower output of the engine. Ideally, you want the engine to peak out at the end of the straightaway. This is where your fastest lap times will occur. If you keep decreasing the number of teeth, your lap times will start to fall off. The engine will not reach its maximum output power.

If you add teeth, you will have more low end power and better acceleration out of the corners, however, you will be giving up some top-end speed, as the engine will peak out before you reach the end of the straight.

Most tracks have more corners than straights, and probably the most important footage on the track is the area after the apex of the corner. You need good mid range RPM to be competitive. So, when in doubt as to which gear to use, always select the higher gear (most teeth). In most races, you will generally be running in a pack and will be unable to make good use of your top-end speed for the biggest part of the race. If you can't break out of the pack, you won't be able to make use of your high speed gearing. A good rule to follow is to run the lowest gear possible, until you start getting passed coming out of the corners. Then go back up one tooth. If you are starting up front, you can gear for high speed.

CLUTCH SETUP

One of the most difficult things to do is tell someone how to set up a clutch. The only right way is with a stopwatch. Run several laps and check your times. Then, remove some weight and run some more laps, and compare your times. Its a slow, long, tedious process, but it's the best way. One way you can tell if the clutch is slipping is to listen to the engine. Due to the loud exhaust of the engine, it's difficult for the driver to hear, but you can ask someone to listen while you're practicing. If the engine sounds like your going a hundred miles an hour, but the kart feels sluggish when accelerating out of the turns, chances are pretty good the clutch is over slipping, and you need to add some weight or change springs.

If the engine seems to boog down coming out of the corners, and making carburetor adjustments doesn't seem to help, you may have too much weight on the clutch.

It may be necessary to readjust the carburetor low-speed needle after making clutch, flex, or gear changes. Run enough practice laps to determine if the change has really helped. Don't be too quick to change things, take your time and don't change more than one thing at a time. Sometimes its best to run a heat race before making another change, just to feel things out.

If you are using an oil clutch insure that you have the proper amount of oil. Do not overfill. Excess oil will rob you of horsepower.

If you only race at one track, the change from week to week will be small, but if you're racing at more than one track, you may have a completely different clutch and flex setting for each track.

DRIVING

The first thing you should realize is that races are not necessarily won by the man with the fastest kart. Driving technique is very important. There are few places on a kart track where top speed is obtainable. Long straights are rare, and usually only serve to link two sharp corners together. Getting around corners quickly, requires good driving technique. A really good driver usually doesn't look as though he is going as fast as he is. His smoothness makes it appear as though he isn't trying as hard as the others on the track. The smoother you become, the faster your lap times will be.

When you go through a corner, you need to get as near as you can to the limit of your karts adhesion, without actually going beyond it, and sliding, or losing control altogether. The fastest driver through a corner isn't the one who skids all over the track. Every movement of the controls, from a dab at the brakes to a twitch of the steering, causes the kart to lose speed. Momentum and inertia are all important. So close are the margins between success and failure, that vital smoothness can win many races.

For every turn, the maximum speed is dependent upon the radius of the turn. The only way to increase the maximum speed through a turn is by increasing the radius of the turn. You can generally increase the radius of the turn. By using the full width of the track,

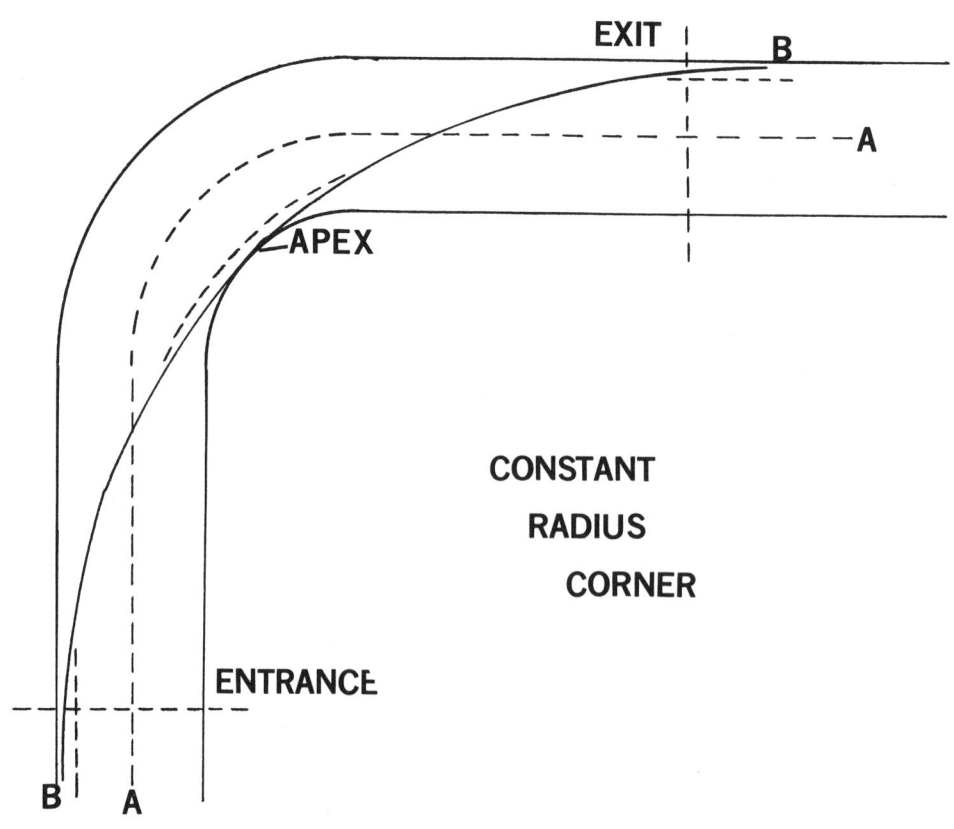

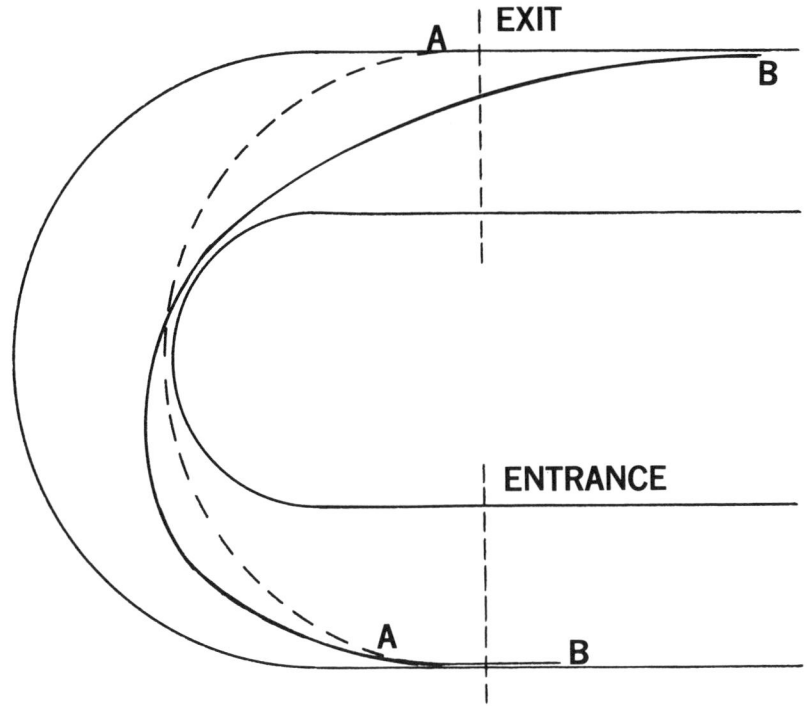

HAIR PIN CORNER

You should brake hard for a corner to allow as much time on the straightaway at top speed as possible. The technique that results in good cornering, is smooth, rapid acceleration, using as much track as possible, to increase the length of the straightaway.

A road racing example that shows the correct technique is presented here. The principles are the same whether driving SCCA Club races, Grand Prix cars, or Karts. In the constant radius turn shown, the maximum speed for path A, on a dry asphalt track is approximately 25 mph. While the larger radius of path B, permits a speed of approximately 41 mph. You can see the advantage of using the entire track.

If you make the mistake of entering or exiting the corner without moving to the outer edge of the track, the radius becomes smaller and maximum speed drops. If you steer one yard wide of the apex, the radius falls even more, and speed falls to 37 mph. You can see the need for smooth consistent cornering techniques. Some drivers try to cut the apex of the corner even closer, and put the inside front wheel actually off the track. If the bend is fast enough, the front wheel will actually be off the ground when you clip the apex. If you look, you will see where some of the grass is worn away from the apex on some corners.

The acceleration capability of our small engines is not good at the high end. It takes a lot longer to go from 8000 RPM to 9000 RPM than it does to go from 1000 to 2000 RPM. You must strive not to scrub off any more speed than necessary.

In some corners, it's not always advantageous to take the path of the largest radius. If the corner is followed by a long straight, it may be more beneficial to alter your line through the corner so as to attain a higher exit speed. A hair pin curve is a good example of this type of corner. If the turn could be taken flat out, path A would be the fastest, because it has the largest radius. However, few hair pin curves can be taken flat out. It becomes necessary to negotiate the curve in such a manner to enable you to take full advantage of the karts acceleration.

To reach a higher speed at the exit of the corner, you must start accelerating as soon as possible while still in the corner. To achieve this, it is necessary to stay wide, and turn, sharper on the approach to the corner. The corner will be taken at a slightly reduced speed, but the kart will be so positioned that maximum acceleration can be applied earlier. The result is that the kart will reach the exit at a much higher speed than a kart following the constant radius path.

Do not attempt to change your path through a corner after you've set up your line. If you slide or slip around, you are turning one corner into a succession of smaller curves, all of which have a radius smaller than the original, consequently your corner speed will drop.

In kart racing, the straights are usually not very long, but you should have time to glance at the heat gauge, or adjust the carburetor. Whatever you do, allow yourself enough time to position the kart for the next corner. Another consideration is some competitors may try to duck inside of you to make you change your line. You may have to change your line to prevent this. It will slow you down somewhat but you will still be in front of him. This occurrence is what can cause a slightly slower karter to pull away from a couple of faster karts who are battling it out. Take care to leave your competitor racing room or you may both be watching the race from the side lines.

THE COMPETITION BEGINS

This chapter is "what it's all about". All the weeks and months of hard work come to a head when you qualify for the race. This chapter will help you under stand qualifying, and help make the job easier.

The section on the race itself explains getting into position for the pace lap, the start, and how to get through the most dangerous part of the race, which is the first turn. It also includes tips on how to improve your position during the race.

Between race activity is also covered. In order to finish in the money, or win a trophy, you have to finish all of the races, so between race check out, is just as important as prerace preparation.

QUALIFYING

Qualifying is very important, but one shouldn't lose sight of its objective, that is, to earn a starting spot in the race. Everyone likes to do well and start up front, but the objective is still to get in the race. If you've prepared the kart well, and made good use of the practice session, there is little left to do. You should prepare yourself mentally so you can concentrate on qualifying, and nothing else. It's too late to change anything now, so just do the best you can.

Before qualifying at a new track, you should check the qualifying procedure. Not all tracks are alike. Some tracks have two qualifying laps, but most have only one. Some flagmen will allow you to wave off one or two laps if you should get off the track, or have obvious engine trouble.

If you wish to wave off a lap, raise your arm well above your head to be sure the flagman sees it. You're the one that loses if he was checking with the time keepers, or something else, and missed your signal. A good indication is to check which flag he's holding. If it's the checker flag, then raise your arm again. If you feel something is wrong, don't stay out on the track, pull into the pits and check it out. They will let you qualify later. If you stay on the track and are obviously having difficulty, the flagman will become disgusted with you, and either wave you into the pits, or make you take a qualifying time you don't really want. If you are unable to qualify during your proper qualifying session, you will most likely be allowed to attempt a qualifying run after the normal sessions are completed. If this happens, be ready when the time comes, or you may find yourself a spectator, instead of a competitor. Some tracks will allow a nonqualifier to start at the tail end of the pack, but you should avoid this if possible. It's a long way to the front from the back, but it is better than watching.

When you enter the track, you should warm up the tires and run one or two hot laps. If you have a temperature gauge you should try and get the temperature up above 300 degrees. If you don' t have a gauge, listen to the engine. When you first go out on the track, the engine is cold and will probably blubber for a lap or two. However, when the engine reaches proper operating temperature, the engine should lean out if it was properly adjusted in practice.

On your qualifying lap itself, you should concentrate on turning a smooth, uniform lap. Try and stay in the groove. When you're first starting out in racing I don't recommend you wave off a lap unless you actually spin, or really get out of shape. It's awfully hard for a rookie to tell what his time will be. Just because you feel a little sloppy, doesn't mean you're doing badly. This feeling occurs sometimes because your going a little faster than you have before. Some people just seem to naturally qualify better than others. Just remember the objective, that's what counts.

Before racing begins there is a drivers meeting. You should attend the meeting even though they do tend to become boring and tedious. Every track is different and there may be a local rule you may be unfamiliar with. Two things you should be sure and clarify at the meeting are; first, on a yellow flag do you close up on the leader or hold your position on the track? Second, when the layover flag (blue w/stripe) is displayed, which side of the track should the slower kart move to. I know you're not going to be lapped, but you may be doing the lapping and you don't want to be involved in an accident with a back marker because you thought he was going to move inside when instead, he moved outside.

THE RACE

When the racing begins you should take the time to study the peculiarities of the starter. It's imperative for you to know when the start will be. If you can detect any mannerism of the starter that will give you some advance knowledge of when the start will come, you can get a jump on the rest of the field.

When it's time for your race to grid move your kart into its proper place. This will enable you and your fellow karters to familiarize yourselves with the starting line-up.

When the O.K. is given, start your kart and move onto the track in a safe manner. Do not pull out into the path of another kart, the race has not yet started. The first thing to do is run a hot lap or two to get the tires up to a good operating temperature. Some tracks do not allow this. Generally, when you return to the track for the race, you will find that the engine will run rich or blubber. If you don't wish to adjust the carburetor during the race, don't readjust it now. After the engine warms to a higher operating temperature(usually three or four laps) the engine will lean itself out. If you adjust the carburetor high-speed needle clockwise during the pace lap, it will be necessary to readjust the carburetor during the race or the engine will over heat and seize,

After a couple of laps, I feel it's a driver's responsability to himself and the other drivers, to seek out the pole setter and take his or her place in the proper starting order. You should know who the pole setter is, and after a couple of warm up laps, he should have a hand in the air so he can be easily located.

If the pole setter sets a very slow pace you will probably hear the engine loading up. With a 2-cycle the only cure for this is to lean out the high speed needle for the start. You will have to richin it back up on the first straight or you will soon be in big trouble.

When entering the final turn before the starting line, it's a good idea to increase the engine RPM. This will enable you to get a better start. You can do this by bliping the accelerator a couple of times while holding the kart speed down with the brake. As soon as it appears that the flagman is going to throw the green flag, get off the brake and on the accelerator. Keep as close as possible to the kart in front of you. Keep your eyes open for a chance to move into the proper groove for the first turn.

The start of the race is probably the most exciting time of all. In kart racing, where so many karts are so evenly matched, the start can greatly determine the finishing order. It's a lot easier to pass at the beginning when everyone is driving at a somewhat reduced pace, than a lap later when everyone is at full speed.

In karting, the man who is first into the first turn has a great advantage. In addition to the satisfaction of having made a good start, he has only to stay ahead of the opposition to win the race. This may sound obvious, but the fact that he will not need to chase or overtake someone, gives him time to concentrate on being smooth and consistent on each lap.

Due to the closeness of kart engines it's possible for a person to snatch the lead at the start in a uncompetitive kart and hang on to it, or even pull away, from a couple of faster karts who are dicing it out, where as he probably couldn't have passed the faster karts had he gotten off to a poorer start.

The biggest hazard at the start is the common occurrence of someone in the pack spinning or slipping sideways and getting hit. It's worth remembering that for the most part, a spinning kart will spin to the outside. So, if someone in front of you spins out, it's a good idea to head to the inside of the track. Look before you dive inside, you may compound the accident by cutting someone else off.

If an accident happens in front of you, you should try and stay on the track if at all possible, even if it means coming to a complete stop. Most tracks have treacherous infields, and once you're in to them, it's nearly impossible to get back onto the track without losing a lot of time. In 2-cycle racing you should try and keep the engine running at all cost. At most tracks if your engine is dead your through for the race. Most tracks will restart the race if there is an accident in the first turn don't panic.

In the first couple of turns, you will probably be forced from the ideal line because of other karts. Keep your wits about you, don't drive over your head. If there's a opening, take it, but remember, a good start helps make for a good finish. However, if you lose control and spin the whole pack will undoubltly pass you, and it is very difficult to make up those positions under full racing speed.

After the first lap or two, most races tend to settle down a little. If you have the power, it's advantageous to improve your position in the early stages of the race. Remember, there is a similarity of power in all kart engines. If you should get stuck behind a slower kart, the leader can build up a sizable lead, and by the time you get an opportunity to pass the slower kart, you'll never be able to catch the leader.

Kart racing is probably the most competitive racing there is. The class system keeps the competition rather equal except for driver ability, kart preparation, and engine preparation. This brings up an interesting question. How do you pass someone who is just as fast as you are? One answer is footsteps. By this I mean, keep the pressure on the kart you're chasing. Stay as close to him as you can without bumping him. Pull along side a little, even if you know you don't have the power to get around him. In other words, let him know you're there. It can be very unnerving, especially for a first year man. When you get close, he'll hear the footsteps, your engine, and start to worry more about keeping you back than about driving his own race, and usually, before long he'll make a minor mistake, and if you're close enough, you'll be able to slip by.

Another way is to follow the kart ahead of you for a couple of laps making a note of the line he follows through each turn. Almost all drivers fall into a pattern. Watch for a corner where he swings wide coming out of a corner, and on the next lap, change your line through that corner to bring yourself inside of your competitor, and try to out accelerate him to the next corner. You should always take the inside line if you can. That way, if you pull up beside him, you will be on the inside for the next corner. As a result, you will most likely be able to steal his line and he will have to give way to you.

There is an unwritten law in all racing that holds true in kart racing. If the overtaking kart is not sufficiently along side the leading kart to assure being seen by the driver, then the turn still belongs to the lead kart.

It is a basic racing fact, that all good drivers use the same basic lines through the same corners. Because of this, the cornering speeds reached by most top drivers are very close to one another. If one of the competitors has more power, he may have the advantage and be able to accelerate out of the corner more quickly. However, since it's more than likely they have similar horsepower, it's very difficult for a driver to pass an opponent on the succeeding straight. The most frequent point for overtaking is in the vulnerable seconds of braking before the next corner. If a driver can use the top speed of his kart for a second longer than his opponent, then he will be able to pass him, even if his kart is no faster. The most common place for a driver to over take is on the inside at the end of the straight.

Karting is expensive business even if you're only in it for the fun of it. The dollars and time spent are a sizable investment. Trying to bump and bang your way through the field will only tear up your equipment, and make you many enemies. There always seems to be some guys who have no regard for their equipment or how they drive. You will soon learn who they are, and will do well to give them plenty of room, if they should be in your race. Fortunately, they are usually ill prepared and are seldom around for the finish. The major concern is that they don't spin out and take you out with them.

Another point I'd like to make is, if it should rain while you're on the track, be very careful. Slick racing tires were designed for maximum adhesion on a dry track, however they have zero traction on a wet track. Proceed to the pits with extreme caution.

If the exhaust header should break, or the pipe becomes disconnected from the header during a race, the engine will have a tendency to run lean. If you continue to run flat out, the engine temperature will rise, if not corrected, and piston seizure can result. If you are near the completion of the race and you wish to finish the event, you will need to richen the high-speed needle, and continue at a reduced speed. If you have a temperature gauge, keep a close eye on it. If you can't keep the engine cooled down, give it up and head for the pits. One race isn't worth the cost of a new engine.

If during the progress of a race, a driver inadvertently comes to a stop on the course in the path of other karts, he should remain in his kart and raise one arm above his head as a signal to other drivers that he is in trouble an will not move his kart, or rejoin the race, until it's safe to do so. Drivers should signal by raising an arm over his head if he intends to stop, pull off the track, or suddenly change his driving pattern.

When two karts are entering a turn together, the kart that is behind, whether it be an inch, or several feet, is required to negotiate the turn without endangering or impairing the progress of the kart in front. Likewise, the kart in front should not deliberately block a competitor.

If you should lose your brakes while on the track during practice, qualifying, or a race, Do Not drive the kart into the pits. So many times I've seen karts tearing through the pits, running over other karts and people. It creates a very dangerous situation. If you lose your brakes, stay on the track until the karts momentum is reduced enough to enable you to safely pull into the infield. If you must stop in a hurry kill the engine, if you have time, and spin the kart into the infield away from any obstacles. If you do not have your kart under control, DO NOT enter the pits!

If your kart becomes disabled during the race, move it far enough from the track so as not to endanger other karters. Do not leave it parked near a corner. Move it to a straight stretch.

Upon returning to the pits at the completion of the race, you must proceed directly to the scales. You must not return to your pit area first. You can be disqualified if you do so. Even if you finished last, you should weigh in. Most tracks only pay points if you finish the race, and weighing is part of the race.

Between races you must prepare for the next race. Check the header bolts and the engine mounting bolts. Check the carburetor mounting nuts. Check them with a wrench, do not just eyeball them. Inspect the throttle linkage. Does the throttle open completely? Is the throttle cable frayed? Check the exhaust pipe. Is it still securely mounted to the kart and header? Walk around the kart and be sure that all the tires and rims are in good shape. Inspect the wheel nuts, are they still in place? Don't forget to refill the fuel tank. Shake the fuel vigorously before adding it to the tank. Inspect the chain. Is it still slack or did it tighten up? If it's tight, you will have to readjust the engine position or make a new chain.

Oil the chain after every race. Check the sprocket, is it still tight?

Now is also the time to evaluate your performance in the last race. Will a gear change help? Remember one more tooth will give you a little more power out of the turns, but you will be giving up a little high-end power. Maybe changing the length of the flex will help. Shorten it for more high-end, lengthen it for more low end. How about clutch weight. Did the kart bog coming off the corners? Remove some weight, or did it slip too much? Add weight. Did the kart handle O.K. in the corners? A little less air pressure in the rear tires will make the rear stick better, more air will let it slide more. Decisions, decisions, now's the time to make them. Remember, you should only make one change at a time. If after all that, you still have time before your next race. take a break and watch the other classes.

After the last race of the day comes the time for the awards. Whatever the award, trophy, plaque, or money, it's nice to go home with a prize. It gives you a feeling of accomplishment. If you win congratulations and a "well done" are in order. Win or lose, it's back to the grind of preparing for the next race.

A field of Baby karts awaiting the green flag. It doesn't matter if your 5 or 55 years old, the trill of competeing is indescribable

The days of racing like this are long gone. But karting is still very much a family and fun sport.

The trill of competeing is the same whether you race on dirt or asphalt, oval or road courses. It all begins when you get in that first kart.

RELATED INFORMATION

This chapter covers related information which includes such things as jackets, driving suits, neck collars and helmets. Information about ear plugs, driving gloves, and shoes are also discussed. Some of the most common rules an regulations are presented. The color and purpose of the starter flags.

A section on miscellaneous tid bits is presented covering such things as engine storage, seat repair, and fire safety.

This chapter also contains an extensive section on the preparation, priming and painting of a kart. Both Epoxy and Irom paint are discussed, so you can intelligently decide which is best for you.

CLOTHING

The wearing of a jacket and helmet is mandatory at all tracks. Gloves and neck collars are required at some tracks and highly recommended at all tracks. No one but a fool would enter the track without them, even for practice. The first time you're on a kart that rolls over you'll be glad you had them.

Drivers are required to wear a drivers suit or a jacket of heavyweight leather or vinyl material and full length pants. Nylon or cotton jackets just won't do the job. A good jacket is cheap protection against track burns if you should get thrown from the kart, or end up with someone's kart in your lap.

Your leather jacket should be cleaned of dirt and oil and treated with one of the readily available leather softeners on the market. This treatment will keep your jacket from becoming brittle and will prevent cracking.

The use of ear plugs is recommended, due to the high note of the engine exhaust. Buy a pair that fit and are comfortable to wear. Buy a couple pairs so that if you lose one, you'll have a replacement. Keep them clean, or you'll run a chance of getting a case of ear infection. Ear plugs reduce only high frequency, so you still hear everything you need to hear. Ear plugs are not required in karting.

Driving gloves are popular also. A good selection is available at most kart and cycle shops. They will protect your knuckles in case of a tumble. Most tracks how require them.

Be sure that your clothing fits tight so that it won't get entangled in the engine or drive train. Some drivers tape their pant legs tight around their ankles to prevent the wind from blowing up their legs, and causing wind drag.

Most karters wear gym shoes for racing. Ordinary street shoes tend to slip off the pedals in the heat of competition.

HELMETS

Good helmets are expensive. The Bell Star and Simpson helmets are unquestionably the best. They are used by virtually all professional race drivers, and are worth their cost. You can, however buy a helmet which will give you adequate protection for a lot less money.

Helmets which have been made in the past three or four years are substantially better than those made earlier. Look for a sticker inside the helmet. It should say "Snell 1990". The Snell sticker indicates that the helmet has passed the Snell Foundation Standards. These standards change from time to time so check with your local track to find out what the latest standard is. Most of the helmets manufactured today are made Kevar, the new carbon fiber material.

A full face helmets protect the face and eyes from stones and rubber thrown from other karts. They also protect you from wind and sunburn. Helmets are available with either clear or tinted shields. The outside structure of the helmet shell must provide full ear protection. A fancy paint job is nice, but it's also expensive.

RULES

The following are some rules which apply at most any track.

The prime responsibility for the safe condition and operation of any kart in competition rests with the driver.

All persons competing in karting events shall maintain a neat appearance.

All fuels and other flammable liquids shall be stored in plastic or metal containers. No glass containers are allowed.

The use of alcoholic beverages and/or illegal drugs is prohibited during any event.

The use of seat belts is prohibited in all classes of sprint racing.

Flarings, spoilers, and wings are being allowed in some sprint classes. Check with your local track.

All weight added to meet minimum kart driver weight requirements shall be bolted to the kart. Carrying of ballast on the driver's person is prohibited. No weight shall be bolted to the underside of the kart.

All karts must be equipped with a chain guard designed to eliminate the possibility of personal injury.

Exhaust systems must be such that exhaust gasses are carried away and rear ward of the driver.

If for any reason, a driver is forced to stop his kart on, or near, the track during an event, it should be his first duty to place his kart in such a manner as to cause no danger or hazardous condition to oncoming competitors.

A driver entering the track, whether from the pits, or the infield, will do so in such a matter so as to cause no danger or hazardous condition to any on coming karts.

Any kart observed to be leaking fuel during an event, be it from the tank, fuel line or vent, shall be immediately black flagged.

No transmission, gearbox or other device which permits a change of gear or sprocket ratios while the kart is in motion is permitted in the sprint classes.

FLAGS

Each competitor is responsible for the knowledge of and adherence to the flags.

GREEN
Displayed at the start of competition or practice, and kept visible as long as the track is clear for racing.

RED
Stop immediately! The track is hazardous and unsafe for racing. Clear the track as soon as circumstances permit. Do not stop so abruptly so as to cause an accident.

YELLOW
Caution, be prepared to stop. Track may be partially blocked by an accident, people, animal or an object which may have fallen off competing vehicles. It means to slow down, and use caution, hold your position. No passing is allowed.

GREEN & YELLOW
Flags rolled and displayed together, indicate a restart. slow and reform the starting line-up for a complete restart.

BLUE
Lay-over Flag. A faster competitor is trying to over take you, move over as safely as possible

GREEN & YELLOW
When displayed crossed they indicate the race is half over.

WHITE
There is one lap to go.

BLACK ROLLED
You are warned your driving is bordering on disqualification and any further display of the same will be cause for disqualification.

BLACK
Reduce your speed and stop at your pit. Any driver who has received the black flag should remember that it may be for a mechanical defect of which he is unaware, and should proceed cautiously to the pits. In QT racing you have run under your time. If you are unsure the flag is for you make another lap. Most tracks quit scoring you when the black flag is givin so ignoring it will not benefit you.

CHECKERED
The race or practice period has concluded.

STORAGE

If you live in a northern state and you are going to put your kart up for the winter, or if you're just giving up racing for a while, here are a few things you should do to prevent damage to the engine.

Nitro-methane and most other zip type additives are quite corrosive, and they will ruin the engine and carburetor if allowed to sit for six months or more. Even gasoline will become gummy after a long period of time, and plug the passageways in the carburetor.

The first thing to do is drain the fuel tank. I then recommend that you remove the engine from the kart. Disassemble the carburetor and flush all the interior parts with plain gasoline. Then take a oil soaked rag and wipe all the parts.

Remove any excess grease from the external surfaces of the engine and wipe it with an oily rag.

The best way to prepare the cylinder is to remove the sparkplug pour an ounce or two of oil in the sparkplug hole, and spin the crank shaft over a few times.

I then recommend you store the engine inside the house if at all possible, to prevent the cold and moisture from getting to it. Remember, it's an expensive racing engine, and even if you never race again, you may want to sell it someday, and recover a part of your investment. A rusted engine isn't worth anything.

SEAT REPAIR

Over a period of years, most kart seats become broken around the mounting holes and some karters wear holes in the bottom of the seat. Most of this damage can be repaired. You can use one of the fiber glass repair kits available from the automotive section of a discount store. Read the directions and follow them.

The most important step in any fiberglass repair is the very first one. The seat must be clean. The fiberglass will not adhere to the seat if it has any oil on it. The filler will flake off when it hardens. Remove all paint, dirt, and oil. All seats have some oil and road deposits on them. Clean it thoroughly and then clean the cleaner off also.

Use the fiberglass cloth supplied with the kit to make the initial repair. Put the first layer of fiberglass on thin. After it hardens, apply a second layer to help strength the repair. After the repair hardens, sand the area smooth and you are ready for a paint job.

SAFETY

Safety begins at home, or more correctly in the garage. Karting require the storage of gasoline or other inflammable fuel from week to week. Care should be exercised so that the fuel cans are not placed near an open flame. It has become popular in many new homes to install the hot water heater in the garage. Beware if you have a gas hot water heater, they have an exposed pilot light. Fumes released while mixing fuels can cause an explosion.

Everyone should have at least one fire extinguisher close at hand at all times. A 2 1/2 pound or larger unit is recommended. A general purpose 2 1/2 pound dry powder type extinguisher sells for less than $20.00 at most stores. It's cheap insurance if you should ever need it. You may not be able to put the fire out, but you should be able to contain it until the fire department arrives. Any extinguisher you buy should bear the UL seal.

Do not place the fire extinguisher in the same general location as the fuel cans. If a fire breaks out, the heat from the fire will prevent you from getting to the extinguisher. Place the extinguisher near a room exit, in a highly visible, and easy to get at place.

Fires are classified in three categories. Class A, ordinary combustibles such as wood or cloth. Class B, flammable liquids, such as gas and oil, and Class C, electrical fires.

If you use your fire extinguisher, aim it at the base of the fire, not at the smoke or flame, use a side to side motion. Many small extinguishers discharge in about 10 seconds, so it's imperative that you get right to the source of the fire. When fighting flammable liquids such as gasoline, don't stand to close, or the force of the spray may spread the fire. After using an extinguisher, it should be recharged by a qualified service center.

If you don't have a fire extinguisher and the fire is relatively small, you may be able to smother it with a blanket, or ordinary table salt. You can use water on class A fires such as wood, paper, or cloth. Do not use water on oil, grease, or electrical fires.

PAINTING

Normally after a few racing seasons, karts tend to become scratched and marred. Most karters start thinking about repainting the old kart. With the cost of new karts so high, one doesn't always have the money to buy a new one, but a new coat of paint can make even an older kart look pretty good. For some reason, a freshly painted kart just seems to run better, even though we know it makes no real difference. Painting a kart is a big task, so you should take time to do it right. I will describe two methods, both of which I have used. The first is a relatively inexpensive epoxy paint, which requires no special equipment or skills to apply. With a minimum amount of abuse, it will last a couple of seasons, and still look reasonably good.

The second is a more professional type of paint called Imron. Imron is a polyurethane air dry enamel, developed and sold by DuPont. It offers a superior gloss retention and maximum chemical resistance. It gives a wet look even after it's dry. It always looks like you just finished painting it. Imron is used by most of the stock car racers as well as fleet truck operators. Its only disadvantage is it's higher cost, and it requires spraying equipment to apply. It is not available in spray cans.

PREPARATION

Before you can begin to paint, you must prepare the kart. The very first thing to do is remove everything from the frame. You just cannot do a respectable job with the floor pan, axle, and other hardware still mounted on the kart. If it can be removed, take it off. It will make the job a lot easier, and you'll have a better looking job when you're done.

The next step is to completely remove all the old paint. The best way to do this is to have the frame sandblasted. To find someone to do the sandblasting, go through the yellow pages of your phone book. You can usually get the job done faster if you pick one of the smaller shops. If you do not want to have the kart sandblasted, you can use one of the many paint removers on the market. It will take a little elbow grease, and most of a day, but you can do the job.

Sandblasting is the bombbarding of the part with sand propelled by high air pressure. The process does not remove any of the parent material if done properly. The main purpose of sandblasting is to remove paint, rust, grease, and oil, in preparation for painting.

I have used both methods, and I have to tell you that sandblasting is a whole lot easier. If you use a paint remover, follow the directions on the can. After applying the remover initially, scrape the paint off with a paint scraper. Then apply another coat of remover and vigorously rub the frame with a wire brush. Use paint removers in a well ventilated place, preferably out of doors. Avoid prolong breathing of the vapors, or skin contact.

If you want to save a few dollars, and still get a good paint job, you can strip all the paint off with a paint remover and then have the frame sandblasted. Most shops will sandblast a bare frame for about half the price of one that's painted. Be sure to mask off any chrome areas which are a part of the frame.

If the frame has been sandblasted you should go over it with a wire brush. This will remove any sand residue that may have become embedded in the frame. If the sand is not removed, it will work itself out during the painting process.

Do not allow the frame to sit around for a extended period of time unpainted or it will rust. The rust will then need to be removed before it can be properly painted. If you don't have the time or money to paint it right away, at least put one coat of primer on it before you stop.

Whenever you paint, whether it's the primer or the cover paint, avoid a excessive build up of material. The part to be painted should be covered in several fine coats. If a thick coat is applied it will surface dry, and the interior paint will not be able to dry because of a lack of air.

PRIMER

The next step is to apply a primer. The purpose of a primer is to bond the paint to the surface being painted, and to prevent corrosion. For the primer to do its job, the surface must be as clean as possible. If the part has not been sandblasted, a good scrubbing with a paint thinner is highly recommended. You should avoid smudging the surface with finger prints. Touching it will add oil to the surface. If you are painting with spraying equipment, use a good grade of lacquer primer, or Corlar Epoxy primer. The first coat should be triple etched. It will help give you better adhesion. The primer should be applied in a smooth, even spray. You should apply at least two coats. Be sure to allow sufficient drying time between applications. The primer should be lightly sanded with a fine grade sandpaper between coats. When finished, the primer should be approximately 2 mils thick. Most paint shops have a gauge to measure the thickness of the paint. Do not use a non-sanding type primer.

I recommend you use zinc chromate primer on anything that you are going to paint by brush or spray can, especially if you are painting aluminum, such as a gas tank. On aluminum parts, the zinc chromate actually bonds itself with the outer layers of the aluminum. On steel, the zinc has a galvanization effect. Galvanizing helps protect against corrosion. Be sure and follow the directions on the label.

EPOXY PAINT

You can paint the kart yourself with one of the many aerosol spray paints on the market. The paint itself should be an epoxy enamel. Epoxy paint is resistant to gasoline, menthol, and other fuel additives. It is also chip resistant under normal wear and tear. No special skill is required. Read the label and follow the directions.

The frame should be painted in a well lighted, well ventilated place, free of dust and air currents. One trick you can use is to hose down the floor with water before you start painting. The room temperature should be at least 70 degrees, so that the paint can cure properly.

I do not recommend that you use a clear acrylic enamel as a final coat, unless you've had previous experience with it. Most claim a high gloss retention and abrasion resistance, however, over the course of a season, I have found that some acrylics discolor and have to be removed.

IMRON PAINT

You should not attempt to paint with Imron unless you are an experienced painter, and have the necessary equipment to do the job properly. Imron is a two part paint. You mix 3 parts Imron with 1 part of a activator. The mixture should be used within 8 hours of mixing. An accelerator can also be added to speed up the drying time. You should first apply a tack coat. Allow it to set up for approximately 20 minutes and then apply a full second coat. When painting the frame you will find that a lower nozzle pressure will probably work best. The objective is to get a even coat of at least 2 mils of paint over the whole frame. You should avoid a build up of paint and primer in excess of 6 mils. If you get too much paint on the frame, it will tend to chip easier. You should not attempt to bake the finish with heat lamps or you may lose some of the high gloss. Imron air dries in 6 to 10 hours and with a accelerator added, it dries in 2 to 4 hours.

HIGH TEMPERATURE PAINT

Some expansion chambers are sold unpainted, and after a few years, if left unprotected, they will begin to rust. I find the best thing to do is paint the chamber with a high temperature paint. Lightly sand the chamber with a fine grade of emery cloth. Clean the chamber of any grease, rust, or dirt. Wipe the surface clean with a good paint thinner. Avoid getting fingerprints on the chamber.

The paint used must be a high temperature paint, 1200 degrees or more. I have used TMP's 1200 plus, Ultra High Temp. Paint with good results. It's fast drying, It air drys in 15 minutes, and the chamber can be mounted immediately. 1200 plus has no paint odor when the pipe is used. Another good high temperature paint is VHT 1200 degree Flame Proof coating.

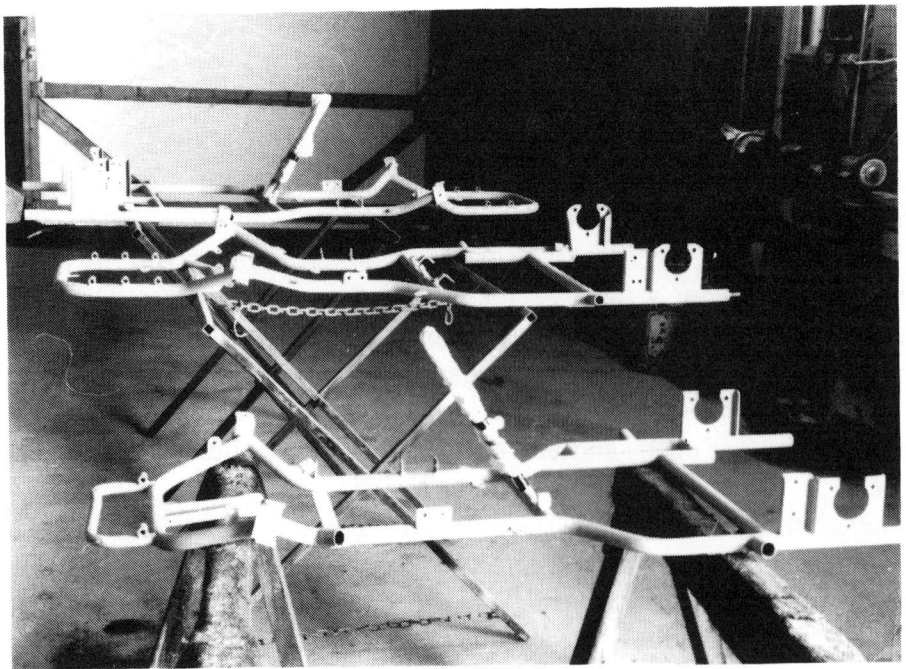

A collection of frames all sandblasted, inspected for cracks and coated with primer. A couple coats of paint and they will be as good as new.

YAMAHA

The Yamaha has become the dominate engine in the 2-cycle classes. It is for this reason I have chosen to include this chapter. I wish to caution you, however, that the material presented here is based on only a few years experience with the engine. It will take several years before all the idiosyncrasies are known. We learn more about the engine every week, keep in mind that this chapter is far from complete, let's just say that it's a beginning. However, I hope it will give you some insight into its performance and maintainability if you elect to purchase this kind of engine.

The Yamaha is a metric engine. If you have metric tools from working on a car or motorcycle, you should be in good shape. If you have no metric tools, you will need to buy some if you purchase a Yamaha. One good thing about the metric system is that screwdrivers, hamners, pliers, and cresent wrenches fit both standards.

The first big decision you will need to make is whether or not to have the engine superstocked, or in other words, Blue printed. If you are going to run IKF or WKA and be competitive, you will most likely have to have it done. If you are just going to run the local tracks, you may be able to get along without it, but I firmly believe, you'll be happier with your engine if you have it done. Have the work done by a reputable shop that has some experience with the Yamaha engine.

The Yamaha engine differs from other 2-cycle engines in that it is a piston port engine. A piston port engine is similar to a reed valve engine, except the piston itself opens and closes the inlet port, instead of using a pair of reeds to accomplish the job. The fuel still enters the crankcase and travels through the transfer passages to the upper cylinder.

The Yamaha engine ignition system is a breakerless, transistor controlled ignition, TCI. It contains no breaker points. The TCI module must be grounded in order for the system to function properly. One common method is to mount the unit on the motor mount. Another popular method is to mount it on the rotor cover. I perfer this method because when you remove the engine it's not necessary to disconnect the module or forgeting to reconnect it.

Do not attempt to run the engine without the TCI module being grounded or the TCI may be destroyed. It's important that the TCI be securely mounted so that it can not vibrate loose during use. The later model engines have an external ground wire which should be securely grounded to the engine or kart frame. Do not shut off the engine by removing the spark plug wire or damage to the TCI unit may result. A kill switch can be wired to the spare terminal on the TCI.

There is a replacment module for the TCI. Its made by ATOM. They actually have several models available. One module is a stock replacement, one which retards the spark above 10,000 rpm, and one that advances the timing 2 degrees. Insure that the module you which to use is legal in your class.

The place where I have found that the Yamaha stands out, is in reliability. You find very few engine related failures. If you canvassed the drop outs from the Yamaha classes, you will find that the majority of the failures were not due to engine related problems, but rather a lack of proper preparation on the part of the driver. I have found over the season, that the Yamaha requires less between race maintenance and has given me more time to work on clutch settings and flex length. I've also had more time to enjoy other races and associate with other karters. I sence a much more relaxed attitude at the track.

I have spent less money on new pistons, rings, bore and hone jobs, than with any other engine. Don't expect the other expenses of racing to disappear just because you purchased a Yamaha, they won't. I think that when all is said and done, you'll find that over the course of a few seasons, the cost of racing is relatively the same no matter which class you participate in. The Yamaha is not a magic solution to the high cost of racing.

The Yamaha offers a slightly different dimension to kart racing. The class requires good skills as a mechanic and driver, to excel. In other classes you have a high attrition rate, but in the Yamaha class, the good guys run good all the time and you have to be just as good or better to beat them on the track. It becomes necessary to pay more attention to smaller details such as kart and engine preparation and driver ability.

The Yamaha classes tend to be much more competitive than many of the other classes, a driver's ability is perhaps more apparent.

The Yamaha should not be run without a chain guard. With the inside mounted clutch, the chain is in a very precarious position. You should mount the guard on the engine or on the kart. Try to avoid attaching the chain guard to both, or the vibration will cause the guard to break.

Mount the TCI module securely to the engine or the motor mount. The module must be grounded for the ignition system to function properly. The newer engines have an external ground wire. Be sure that it is also grounded. The TCI module is very expensive and it can be instantly destroyed if the ground connection is allowed to break while the engine is running.

Care should be exercised to run the high voltage lead to the spark plug so that it does not come in contact with the head. The vibration of racing can cause the insulation to wear through and cause the engine to misfire. If you run the lead through the special ring supplied with the engine, you should put a liberal amount of electrical tape around the lead.

The Yamaha engine seems to require a in-line fuel filter. The Walbro carburetor is much more temperamental to dirt than other types of carburetors. Be sure to seal the fuel line at the filter to prevent air leaks. If you do not use a fuel filter, check the filter screen in the carburetor after every couple of races.

Do not use fuel line to replace the tubing for the pulse hose. Use windshield wiper hose, or another similar type hose, since the hose must have a thick strong side wall. If fuel line is used, the vacuum from the engine crankcase can collapse the line and restrict the pressure to the carburetor. This is especially true on a very hot day.

One thing that you may wish to do or have done, is add RTV to the magneto coil where the wire exits the coil. This will prevent the wires breaking from the vibration during a race. The magneto coil is accessible by removing the cover on the side of the engine. The cover can be removed by removing four Allen screws. Some covers are easily removed, but others fit very tightly. If the cover is tight it should be removed with a puller. If you look, you'll see that two of the cover screw holes are taped. If no puller is available, there is another less desirable method to remove the cover. Take two metric M8 screws and file the very end of the screw flat so that they have no burrs. Start the screws into the cover. Turn the cover clockwise as far as possible and hold it there with one hand. This will prevent the threads in the crankcase from being damaged. Alternately, tighten the two screws until the cover is free of the bearing. Remove the ignition coil and place liberal amount of RTV around the point where the wires exit the coil.

The Yamaha timing can be controlled slightly by the air gap between the stator and the rotor. The wider the gap the more retarded, later, the timing will be. The narrower the gap the more advanced, earlier the timing. Don't make the gap to wide or the intensity of the spark will be reduced. The spark intensity or voltage is what controls ignition timing in a TCI ignition. When the gap is small voltage builds up faster and trips the ignition, as the gap widens voltage builds up slower delaying the spark. This same type of thing happens when you move the coil on the mounting screws. It is also the reason the rule book states, any means taken to alter the coil position is illegal. It also says ignition keys must fill slots in crankshaft and rotor. This is to prevent altering the timing by use of half keys, offset keys or no keys at all.

Reinstall the magneto coil and set the flywheel gap. Place a 0.020 feeler gauge under the two outside legs of the coil. Then press down while rotating the coil counter clockwise, and tighten the coil screws. Reinstall the engine side cover.

CARBURETOR ADJUSTMENT

As in the adjustment of any carburetor, the first thing that needs adjustment is the metering lever. For proper adjustment. first remove the diaphragm cover and the diaphragm. The metering lever should be 0.050 inch below the body of the carburetor. The lever can be bent slightly to obtain this setting. When reinstalling the diaphragm, be sure that the diaphragm, plate fits into the fork like end of the metering lever.

Preliminarily, set the low speed needle to 7/8 of a turn out and the high speed needle to 1 turn out. Start the engine and take it out on the track and warm it to proper operating temperature. In small increments, turn the high speed needle out until the engine begins to run rough down the longest straightaway, then turn it back in 1/8 turn. Then run the engine at a slow speed, about the speed of a pace lap. The engine should run clean without loading up. If the engine loads up, turn the low speed needle in about 1/16 turn at a time. Be sure to run a fast lap or two between adjustments to clean out the engine. Remember, if you change the low speed needle, you will have to reset the high speed needle. If the needles don't seems to have the proper range it may be necessary to readjust the fulcrum arm height. If the engine is running to lean the fulcrum arm should be raised. If the engine is running rich the fulcrum arm should be lowered. There is a Yamaha measuring gauge available from most kart shops.

Quickly accelerate the kart from an idle position, and the engine should accelerate cleanly. If you suspect the engine is starving, partially block the throat of the carburetor briefly. If the engine runs better, it needs more fuel. If the engine runs worse, the engine is loading up and the high speed needle should be turned in. Fuel for acceleration is supplied by the high speed needle.

If you are having trouble adjusting the

carburetion on the Walborn carburetor you should check the fuel pump diaphragm. The flapper valve has a tendency to be pulled into the passageway. There are now replacement gaskets available that are of better quality. Inquire about them at your local kart shop.

CYLINDER REMOVAL

After several race days you notice a drop in horsepower. This can be cause by wear of the piston ring. You may also need to replace the ring on/or piston if you have over temp. the engine. Some times this just cause a flash stick and can be repaired by changing the ring. Replaceing the ring and piston is not a difficult job. First, remove the head by removing the six head bolts. With the head removed, you can remove the four recessed bolts that secure the cylinder. After the cylinder has been removed, you can see that the damage is an repair it as necessary. The piston wrist pin is retained by a pair of spring clips, one on each side of the pin. When the clips are removed, the wrist pin will slide out of the piston. The connecting rod bearing has two brass washers on either side. Be sure these are in place when installing the piston. If you examine the piston, you will see a small cut out for the ring pin. This pin must be positioned toward the intake port or carburetor. If it is mounted incorrectly, The ring may catch in the exhaust port and damage the engine.

The retaining clips should be replaced whenever the engine is torn down. After repeated use, the ears become weak and may break off. They can cause damage to the cylinder wall. Replacing the clips can be a lot cheaper than a bore job and a new piston. Make sure that the clips are snapped into the groove in the piston. Replace any gaskets that are damaged. Reassemble the cylinder with the carburetor to the front, and replace the head. Tighten the head bolts in an alternating pattern. Torque them. It will also be necessary to reconnect the short hose for the carburetor pulses from the crankcase.

If you split the crankcase halfs for any reason make note of the fact that two of the retaining bolts are longer than the rest. The longer bolts go into the two holes at the top.

Troubleshooting the Yamaha engine is not that much different than any other 2-cycle engine. The two best diagnostic aids you have are the spark plug and the Air pressure checker. The Yamaha can be air checked the same as any other 2-cycle engine. You may have to purchase, or make a couple of adapter plates, to fit the engine, but the principles are the same.

If you have electrical problems, remove the spark plug and check for spark. Remember that the engine must be turning over pretty fast to fire. If the engine doesn't fire, change the spark plug first. If the plug is O.K. you can test the magneto coil with a ohm meter. Remove the high voltage wire from the spark plug and disconnect the TCI module. Measure from the spark plug wire to ground. The ohm meter should indicate greater than 10,000 ohms. Measure from the small ignition wire to ground. The meter should indicate approximately one ohm. If any of these readings are incorrect, the ignition coil, or the coil wires, are at fault. If the coil is 0.K. you can check the TCI module. Measure from the wire (red lead) to ground (black lead) with the meter set on the R x 10 scale. The meter should indicate approximately 50 ohms. If a different meter scale is used, the readings will vary. Now, reverse the leads. Black lead to wire, Red lead to ground. The meter should read approximately 200 ohms.

If the meter reads an open or a short during either of these tests, it is quite likely something is wrong within the TCI module.

US820

If you are considering competing in the US820 class I recommend you check it out very carefully. Go to a track and watch a few races. Check out how many karts are paritcipating in the class, talk to the drivers and generally keep your eyes open.

I have talked to some karters in this class and they do seem to like the engine, however in this area the fields are small and the attriction is high. One karter told me how much he liked the class, fifteen minutes later, he was loading up and heading home, before the days racing had began. That doesn't sound like fun to me.

The WKA and IKF are trouting this as a entry level class and are trying hard to make it work. Frankly I have a lot of trouble with that. I started my karting career with a West Bend 820. I went through a lot of pistons, and chased a lot of air leaks. I spent more time working on the engine than I did racing. Karting doesn't have to be that way anymore. A beginner needs to spend more time on the track racing and less time working at keeping the engine running.

While the US820 is a good engine, it's still a 2-cycle reed valve engine with a tillotson carburetor. This is just more complicated than a rookie needs, even with the restrictions. Another bad aspect is that parts are not as plentiful as Briggs and Yamaha part are.

Granted you will gain a lot of experence and hard work running this class, but I have to question its real value to your karting future.

I feel this is not the place for a beginner. If you start in US820 and then elect to move up to Yamaha or Briggs, you will need to buy, and learn, another engine and clutch. All a rookie is going to learn in US820 is how to work on an engine, which may be obsolete by the time he learns how to make it reliable. Karting has two of the best entry level classes available in 4-cycle box stock and restriched Yamaha for 2-cycle. It's much more practical to start with a Yamaha or a Briggs. You can then move up in class and still use the same engine and experience. You haven't wasted a couple of years learning an engine you will never use again, or spending money on parts and accessories which you will have no further use for.

Due to the low turn out of karts with US820 engines these karts will be combined with another class, were it may or may not be competitive.

If you feel this is the class for you don't let my opinion detour you. I just want you to go into this with your eyes open. I want you to become a happy, satisfied karter not a disapointed one. Remember this is only my opinion. I only caution you to check it out throughly before you spend your money.

If you really want to go 2-cycle racing many tracks are now running the Yamaha with a can muffler. Most tracks are running both junior and adult classes. IKF calls this class Jr. & Sr. Sportsman. This is a very good place to start a 2-cycle career.

If in the future you want to move up you need only change the box muffler to a tuned exhaust and away you go.

TROUBLE ANALYSIS

Most rookie karters haven't yet gained sufficient information to attempt any serious engine work, but you don't have to be a trained mechanic, or even mechanically inclined, to change a spark plug. The number one cause of the 2-cycle engine not starting is a fouled plug.

This chapter gives a very detailed step by step procedure for troubleshooting a 2-cycle engine. Almost any problem can be found and resolved with some patience and understanding of the engine.

A section is also included on pressure checking the engine. Pressure checking is a very revealing diagnostic aid and you should understand how to take advantage of it.

Piston seizure is something that is familiar to all 2-cycle engine owners. To the new karter though, you may only know that the engine quit. This section will help you recognize it for what it is and the ways to prevent it.

There are four flow charts, located in the next few pages. Select the symptom that best represents your problem and use that chart. Each block of the flow chart has a diagnostic test to perform. After performing the test, follow the path out of the block which corresponds to the results obtained in the test. Follow the steps through the flow chart until the trouble is located, If you don't know the proper procedure for performing the test indicated, refer to the appropriately numbered paragraph in the accompanying text for that trouble chart.

If the engine still fails to operate upon completing all the steps in the flow chart, the only remaining thing to do is air check the engine. If the pressure check reveals any problems, repair the leak and attempt to start the engine. If the engine still fails to run properly it's time to pack it up and take it to the local kart shop, or contact someone else who has experience in working on your type of engine.

When taking a engine in for any kind of work, be sure its clean. Some places will, and rightfully so, charge extra to clean it. Take the engine in completely assembled so that the shop will have all the necessary parts. If you take it in and some of the parts are missing, the shop will have no choice but to charge you for them. Don't make the job more expensive than it has to be.

There are some repairs that even a rookie can make. One of these is replacing a blown head gasket. A blown head gasket can be changed at the track, if necessary, if some degree of care is exercised. The two most common causes for a blown head gasket is that the head bolts were not properly torqued upon assembly, or an over heated engine. Remove the head bolts and any other miscellaneous hardware. Before installing the new gasket, carefully inspect the top of the piston and cylinder wall for any damage. If the engine had seized its a good idea to remove the piston and insure that the ring or rings are free in their grove. If the piston is damaged, do not attempt to run the engine until it has been replaced. If your inspection reveals no damage, install the new head gasket and reinstall the head. Torque the head bolts to the proper specification for your engine.

If your engine has an aluminum head gasket it must be replaced. The aluminum gasket will take an impression from the mating surfaces of the cylinder head and the cylinder block when the head bolts are tightened. If the gasket is reinstalled in a different position than its original position, it may not seal properly, even when the head bolts are torqued to their correct value. A leaking head gasket will become blackened in the area of the escaping gases.

On some engines the head bolts are different lengths, insure you return them to their correct position.

PRESSURE CHECKING

Pressure checking your engine can save you money. The 2-cycle engine requires a sealed crankcase in order to develop the pressure and vacuum necessary to perform properly. If the crankcase develops a air leak, the engine will run lean. As a result this will cause the cylinder head temperature to rise and almost always, lead to piston seizure. One early warning sign of an air leak is that the engine will not idle properly and attempts to run faster and faster. The engine should be pressure checked at least once a month. It's not a difficult task to air check an engine. There are kits on the market today that adapt to any engine. It's not uncommon to see someone air checking an engine at the track if the engine has symptoms of running lean.

The pressure check kit includes adapter plates to seal off the exhaust port and the intake manifold. In most cases it is necessary to remove the exhaust header, carburetor, and reed block if you have a reed engine. The kit has a pressure gauge and a rubber bulb, similar to ones used on blood pressure units. Install the adapter plates and tighten the nuts and screws. Pump the pressure up to 7 or 8 pounds and close the air valve. Don't pump the pressure over 10 or 12 pounds or you may damage the crankcase seals. If the engine is new or has a good seal, it should hold the pressure for at least 3 minutes. If the pressure won't pump up, or escapes to fast, you have an air leak. Locating the leak can be done by ear

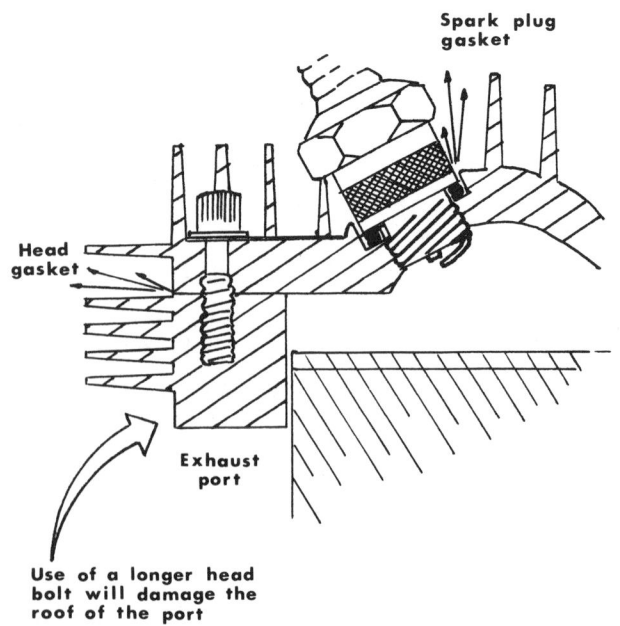

SOME SOURCES OF AIR LEAKS

if the leak is of considerable size. Normally, though, it will require some soapy water, or some very light oil, applied to the seals or gaskets suspected of leaking. The engine should maintain at least 5 pounds for 3 minutes. Most new engines will, however, if you're testing a used engine, it shouldn't lose more than one pound a minute. If it does it needs immediate attention. If the engine won't hold pressure, the first thing to check is the pressure checking equipment itself.

Check the hose fittings and the intake and exhaust adapter plates for a good seal. Usually, the most common air leak is the crankshaft seals and the mating surface between the crankcase halves. If these items check out and the engine still is not air tight, the problem could be in the head gasket or spark plug gasket. If the engine still leaks, the problem must be in the cylinder casting itself. In either case, it's not a job for an amateur and you should seek some professional help.

Pressure checking your engine is cheap insurance. It's a lot cheaper to buy a gasket or a seal, than to have to repair the damage of a seized piston, which may require a bore job and a new piston.

PISTON SEIZURE

Piston seizure is something we all seem to experience sometime during our years of karting. Just about the time you think everything seems to be running real good, the engine quits.

From a technical aspect, the primary cause of piston seizure is the reduction of the cylinder clearance, either generally, or locally, due to piston expansion and cylinder distortion. This is generally caused by the failure or lack of adequate lubrication. The lack of lubrication causes friction which produces heat, which in turn causes more lubrication break down until metal-to-metal contact occurs, then, the piston seizes with the cylinder, and the engine stops.

One of the warning signs of impending seizure is a loss of power, but in most cases, by the time the problem is diagnosed, the cycle is irreversible. The most common reflex is to remove your foot from the throttle, which in reality, only compounds the problem by shutting off what supply of lubrication there was. The correct thing to do is choke the carburetor by hand immediately, forcing it to pump more fuel and oil. This will help cool the engine. Readjust the carburetor as soon as possible. Another sign of impending seizure is you can hear the engine start making a unusual mechanical sound, its a rattling sound.

The two most common causes of piston seizure are mis-adjustment of the carburetor needles, or an air leak.

There are two degrees of seizures, one is a mild seizure which is sometimes called a flash, or quick stick, and the second, of course, is the more catastrophic type. A quick stick usually only requires a ring job to repair the engine, and if it was quick enough, you may be able to finish out the day. Before you try and restart the engine, you should inspect it for possible damage.

A good indication of the condition of the rings can be obtained by checking the compression. Try to spin the engine over with your hand. If the engine turns over, that's one good sign that the damage may not be too extensive. If the crankshaft refuses to move, you've got serious problems. Next, remove the header and take a good look at the piston and the cylinder wall through the exhaust port, If the piston is not broken, and the rings are free in the grooves, you can most likely finish out the day.

If you are running a stock 4-cycle Briggs even a quick stick is usually disastrous. Stock Briggs pistons will crack or break around the wrist pin area. Remove the piston and carefully inspect this area before continuing.

Readjust the carburetor for a richer mixture before you attempt to restart the engine. If the compression is down, you will notice some loss of power on the low end. If the rings are frozen in the piston, or the piston crown is damaged, don't attempt to run the engine until its been rebuilt. It will most likely need a bore job and a new piston, which means a trip to the kart shop.

After completion of the day's racing, the engine should be given a complete checkout. The cylinder should be honed and new rings installed.

After several hours of racing, you may find that the engine lacks low-end power and some of the old zip it used to have. Engines do get old and tired, especially if you've seized the engine a couple of times, and repaired it yourself. You will probably find that the engine will not build up good compression, even after installing new rings. Fortunately, there is a cure for most engines. The problem is most likely in the block. The bore of the cylinder tends to become out of round or egg shaped. If the cylinder is warped, the rings cannot seat properly, and the engine will not have the same "snap" it had when it was new. The egg shape distortion is caused by the intense heat of the exhaust gases on one side of the cylinder, and the cooling temperature of the inlet gases on the opposite side. The conditions are compounded whenever the engine is over heated and the piston seizes.

If you do a lot of racing, it may be necessary to have the engine rebuilt during the course of the year. The kart shop can measure the bore and determine if a bore job is necessary. They can true up the cylinder, fit a new piston, and put the engine back in tip-top shape.

When breaking in a engine with a new piston, or piston rings, run the engine with a rich carburetor setting. Avoid sustained high RPM or low speed running. After approximately one half hour of mild running, allow the engine to cool, and then run another half hour at a slightly faster pace. This should be a adequate break-in period. Do not use any special additives in the fuel during the initial break-in period, as the additives may glaze the cylinder wall and prevent the rings from seating.

ANAEROBICS

The strongest bolt in the world is worthless if it can't be kept tight. Racing vibration, temperature changes and stress will inevitably loosen any bolt that isn't locked in place by some means. Lockwashers have a tendency to damage the aluminum used on most karts and kart engines. Cotter pins, or safety wiring should be used to prevent the nut from coming off, should it become loose. When this is not possible Anaerobics is the answer.

Anaerobic compounds harden into a tough plastic when they contact metal in the absence of oxygen. The plastic solidifies in the microscopic pores of the metal, so that the parts will resist accidental loosening, but can still be removed with ordinary tools. For maximum adhesion, the two surfaces should be as clean as possible. Loctite makes a commercially available primer called Klean-N-Prime, which works very well. When using Loctite or any other anaerobic product, read the directions and follow them.

There are several anaerobic products on the market today. Undoubtedly, the most popular is loctite, or lock-it, manufactured by the Loctite Corporation. However, the brand is not important, what is, is that you use it. It's cheap insurance against mechanical failures.

Anaerobics are color coded by strength. The custom of color coding started with Military Specification requirements and has largely been carried over into commercial use. In general, low strength is indicated by a PURPLE color. Normal strength is BLUE, and provides better vibration resistance than most other locking methods including lockwashers, but will still allow for easy disassembly. Blue is the most commonly used type in karting. GREEN indicates medium to high strength and is used for permanently assembled parts. RED indicates high strength and provides extremely high vibration resistance. Red can be used to repair studs in the intake manifold, or seating a loose crankshaft bearing in the end cover.

ENGINE WILL NOT START

If the engine will not start, the first thing to determine is if the engine has fuel and spark. Without either, the engine will not run.

Step 1. You can usually tell if the engine is firing or not by listening to it. It will cough, or even attempt to run. If it appears that the engine is firing, the problem is probably fuel related. Proceed to the fuel system test, step 13. If the engine appears dead, the problem is probably in the electrical system. Proceed to the electrical system test, step 2.

Step 2. The first place to look for an electrical problem is the ignition kill switch, if you have one. Is it in the run position?

Step 13. The first place to look for a fuel problem is the fuel shut off valve. Don't assume that just because you turned it on, it's still on. Sometimes in the excitement of getting started, someone trying to help may have shut it off. Check it.

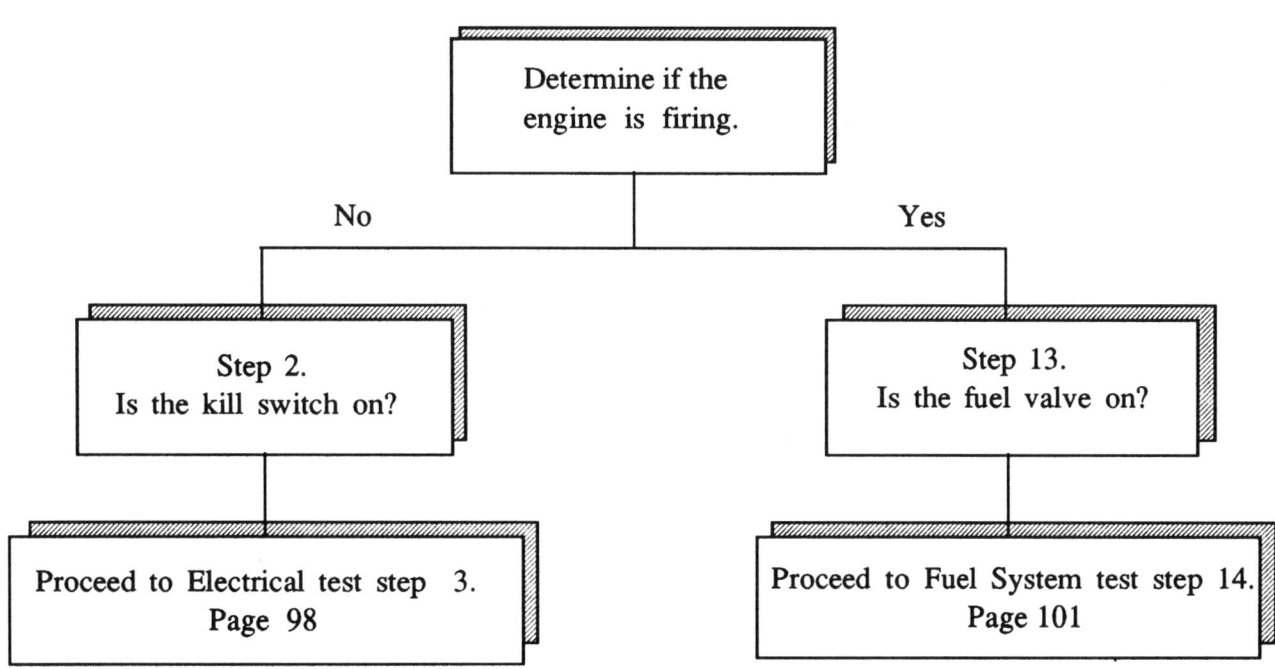

ELECTRICAL TEST

Step 3. The number one cause of ignition failure is a fouled plug. To determine if the plug is fouled remove and inspect it. If the plug is coated with fuel, it's fouled and should be replaced. Another indication of a fouled plug, is fuel dripping out of the exhaust header or flex pipe. If the plug is not fouled, proceed to step 4. If the plug is fouled it should be replaced. Before installing a new plug, it will help make the engine easier to start if you blow the excess fuel from the combustion chamber. Shut the fuel off, and spin the engine over with the starter several times. This will also help prevent the new plug from becoming fouled before it has a chance to start the engine. Install the spark plug. Try to start the engine with the fuel still turned off. As soon as the engine starts, turn the fuel on.

Step 4. If the plug is not fouled, the next step is to check for spark at the spark plug. Without installing the plug, connect the spark plug wire to the top of the plug. Position the plug so the body of the plug comes in contact with the cylinder head. Keep your fingers away from the electrode of the plug. Spin the engine over a couple of times and see if the plug fires. If it does fire, a large blue spark will appear. If it does, the problem is most likely not in the electrical system, but probably in the fuel system. You should proceed to step 14. If the plug fails to fire, the first thing to do is replace the spark plug with a new one and repeat this step. If the new plug fires, install the new spark plug and attempt to start the engine. If the new plug fails to fire, proceed to step 5.

Step 5. The next place to look for the problem is to inspect the ignition wires, check for shorted or broken wires. If the wires are damaged repair or replace them. If the wires are O.K. proceed to step 6.

Step 6. Inspect the magneto coil for damage. Check the coil for proper mounting. Is the coil tight on the engine? The mounting bosses sometimes break. Is the ground wire connected to the mounting bolt? Check the coil lamination to flywheel gap, it should be approximately 0.012 inch. Reset if necessary.

Step 7. The coil can be checked electrically using a VOM. This is a general test that should work for most coils. You may wish to ask your dealer for the exact readings for your engine. Set the meter to the Rx1 scale. Connect the meter leads across the primary windings of the coil (point or transistor side of the coil). The resistance here is very small, on the order of 0.5 ohms, so your meter will most likely indicate a short. This reading is normal, since few meters can read resistance of less than 1 ohm. Connect the VOM across the secondary (spark plug wire). Set meter on Rx100. The resistance should be approximately 6000 ohms. If the coil checks bad, it should be repaired or replaced.

Step 8.   Inspect the flywheel. It should be tight on the crankshaft. If it's loose for any reason, pull it off and inspect the crankshaft key. Sometimes the key will shear off. Check the magnets in the flywheel with a screwdriver. Hold the screwdriver so that the tip is about 1/2 inch away from the magnets. The force of a good magnet should grab the tip. If the magnets have lost their magnetism the flywheel should be replaced. When reinstalling the flywheel, be sure to torque the crankshaft nut.

Step 9.   Does your engine have point ignition? If so proceed to step 11.
If you have electronic ignition proceed to step 10.

Step 10.   Check the ignition module for damage. Check to insure that the module still has a good ground. Is the ground wire connected? If not repair or replace it.

Step 11.   To locate a problem with point ignition it will be necessary to remove the flywheel. Remove the point cover if the engine has one. Rotate the crankshaft and observe the point action. The points should open and close. If the points are not opening and closing, the most probable causes are: misadjusted, burnt, or broken point contacts. A worn rubbing block can also cause the problem. Inspect the point contacts. If they are worn, pitted, or broken replace them. Insure that the point wire is still connected to the points and is not broken.

Step 12.   Next check for bare or frayed wires which could cause a short. The most probable place for a short is where the point wire is connected to the points. Inspect this area carefully. If no short is found repeat step 4 to verify that a problem does indeed exist.

ELECTRICAL SYSTEM FLOW CHART

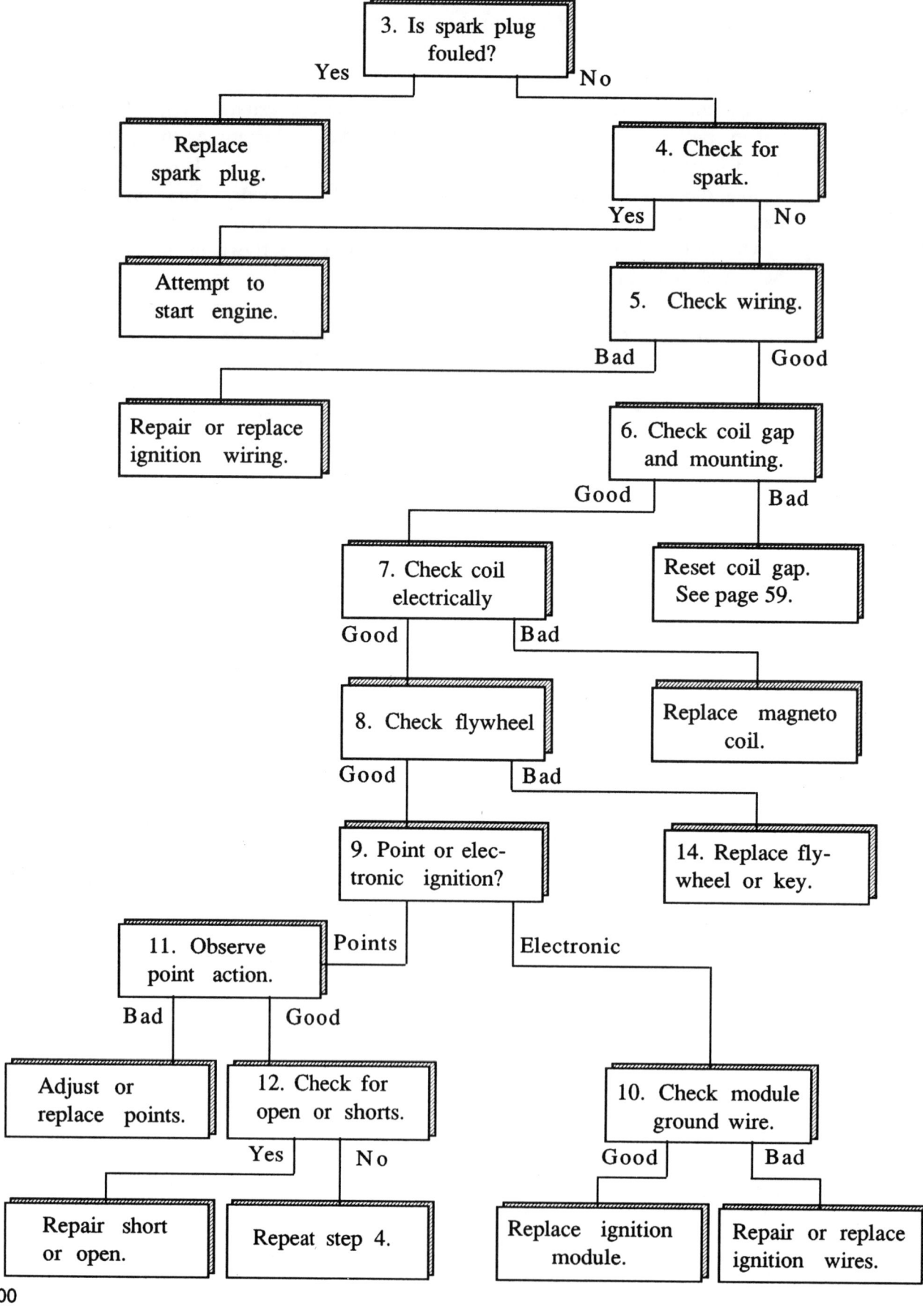

FUEL SYSTEM TEST

Step 14. Look into the throat of the carburetor. If the carburetor is pumping fuel, the throat should have some fuel in it. If the throat is dry, proceed to step 17. If the carburetor has fuel, it will be necessary to determine if the fuel is getting into the engine.

Step 15. Remove the spark plug and inspect its tip for fuel. If the plug shows signs of getting fuel, moist tip, repeat step 4. If no fuel can be detected in the cylinder, proceed to step 16.

Step 16. The only things that can prevent fuel from getting from the carburetor to the cylinder are: reeds on a reed engine, or an air leak. Disconnect the carburetor and remove the reed block. Inspect the reeds for chips or frayed ends. Also look for wrapped or stuck pedals, replace any damaged reeds. If everything else checks out, the next best thing to do is air check the engine.

Step 17. If the throat of the carburetor is dry, look at the fuel line and determine if it contains fuel. If the line has fuel, proceed to step 20. If the line has air in it, it will be necessary to choke the carburetor until the fuel is pumped into the carburetor.

Step 18. Attempt to start the engine again. While the engine is turning over, place your hand over the front of the carburetor and force it to pump fuel. Don't choke the engine too long if it's pumping fuel, or you'll flood the engine and foul out the plug. If the carburetor now has fuel and the engine still doesn't start return to step 14.

Step 19. If there is still no fuel in the line, check the gas tank. Does it have gas in it? If you have gas in the tank, but none in the line, the problem is probably the filter screen on the fuel shut off valve inside the tank. Other possibilities are a plugged fuel filter or a plugged vent hole in the gas cap.

Step 20. If the fuel line indicates that the carburetor is getting fuel, but none is getting to the throat, the problem has to be in the carburetor. The two most logical places are the fuel inlet screen in the top plate, or the fuel inlet lever is not opening the inlet needle. In any case, shut off the gas and inspect the interior of the carburetor for dirt or a broken diaphragm.

NOTE: If the engine has been flooded it may be necessary to replace or clean the spark plug several times. It's best to leave the fuel shut off. There will be plenty of fuel in the crankcase to start the engine. A freon type of solvent can be used to clean a fouled plug.

FUEL SYSTEM FLOW CHART

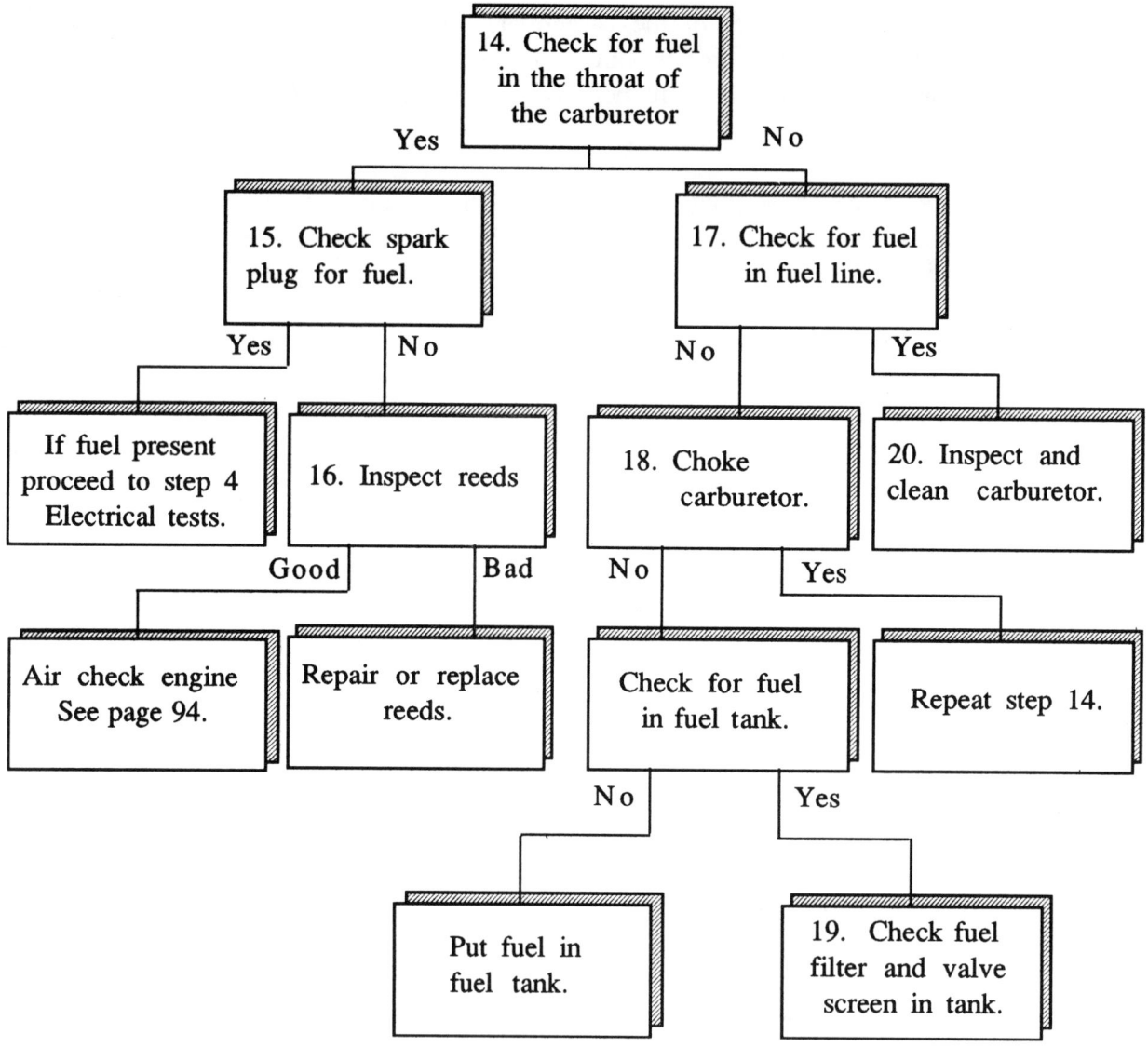

ENGINE WILL NOT IDLE

The engine starts, but will not idle, you can keep the engine running as long as you pump the throttle. If when you remove your foot from the throttle the engine dies. Proceed to step 6. If the engine won't idle, but instead tries to run faster and faster, the cause is almost always an air leak. Proceed to step 1.

Step 1. Before air checking the engine, check for a loose spark plug washer. If you use a heat gauge, inspect the thermocouple washer for damage. Check to insure that the carburetor has not vibrated loose.

Step 2. Check for a sheared flywheel key.

Step 3. On a 4-cycle Briggs check the carburetor body around the mounting flange for cracks, this is a very common failure.

Step 4. If you have a reed valve engine inspect the reeds. A broken or chipped reed is the same as an air leak.

Step 5. If everything checks out O.K. you will need to air check the engine.

Step 6. Check the fuel line for air in the line. If you see bubbles in the line you have an air leak in the fuel system. Inspect both ends of the fuel line for an air tight connection. It's much easier for the carburetor to pump air than fuel. Check the carburetor top cover screws to insure that they are tight.

Step 7. The most common cause for a engine not idling is a defective spark plug. Replace the spark plug even through it may not appear to be fouled.

ENGINE WILL NOT ACCELERATE

The engine starts and idles, but whenever you step on the throttle the engine dies.

Step 1. First, check the fuel lines for bubbles. Air may be leaking into the system if the connections are not tight. It's much easier for the carburetor to pump air than fuel. Check the carburetor top cover screws to insure that they are tight.

Step 2. Are the needle valves still in the carburetor? Is the hardware on the needle valves correctly? The most probable cause is an improperly adjusted carburetor. Check the high speed needle adjustment. Depending on your engine it should be set at 1 or 1 1/2 turns out.

Step 3. Take the covers off the carburetor and check for dirty or partially blocked fuel screens. Inspect the flapper valves to insure that they are pliable and have not been sucked into the passageways.

Step 4. On reed valve engines inspect the reeds for damage. Insure that the reeds seal off the ports. Hold them up to the light and see if you can see through them.

ENGINE RUNS ROUGH, OR VIBRATES EXCESSIVELY

Step 1 Inspect the motor mount bolts. The engine may merely be loose on the mount, or the mount may be loose on the kart.

Step 2 Inspect the flywheel to see if it has sheared the flywheel key. This will cause the engine to be out of time. Inspect for broken fins on the flywheel. This will cause the engine to be out of balance.

Step 3 If everything else checks out, remove the clutch cover and inspect the shoes or disc for broken or damaged parts.

Step 4 If the engine still has a tendency to pop or vibrate excessively the most probable cause is that the engine is out of time. If the engine has been recently worked on, there is a good possibility the timing has slipped.

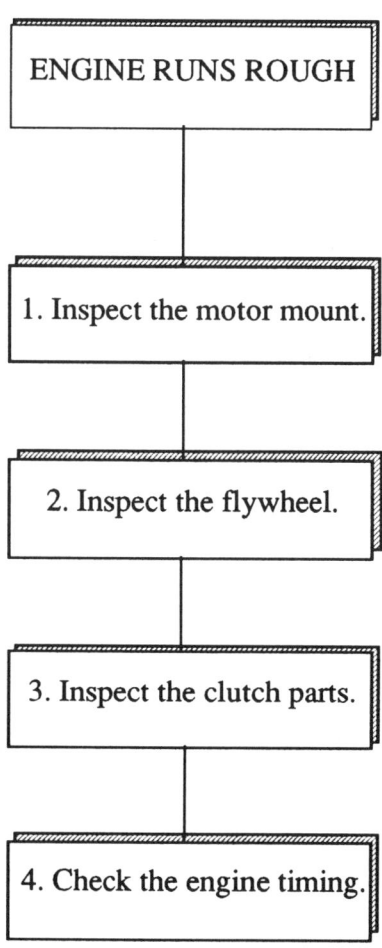

Personal Performance Record

By keeping a record of your performance you will have a record of your kart setup and qualifying time at each track you attend. This will help you should you return to that track again. A performance record also gives you something to look back on at the end of the year so you can evaluate the seasons performance.

Date						
Track						
Qualifying Time						
Race 1						
Race 2						
Race 3						
Setup Notes (gear ratio)						

Date						
Track						
Qualifying Time						
Race 1						
Race 2						
Race 3						
Setup Notes (Gear ratio)						

Additional Reference Material

KARTING
Leroi Smith
Arco Publishing Co, Inc. NY. NY.

KARTING CHALLENGE
Edward Radlauer
Childrens Press, Chicago

KART RACING (Juvenile)
Jerry Leonard
Julian Messner, New York

MOTORCYCLE REPAIR MANUAL
Bob Greene
Peterson Publishing Co.

REPAIR & MAINTENANCE OF SMALL GASOLINE ENGINES
George R. Drake
Reston Publishing Co., Inc.

THE COMPLETE BOOK OF KARTING
Dick Day
Prentice-Hall, Inc. Englewood Cliffs, N.J.

TWO-STROKE POWER UNITS - Their design and application
P.E. Irving
Hart Publishing Co, Inc. NY, NY.

TWO-STROKE TUNER'S HANDBOOK
Gordon Jennings
HP Books, Tucson, Ariz.

ENGINE FUNDAMENTALS
Intertec Publishing Corp.
Overland Park, Kansas

RACING THE YAMAHA KT100S
Jean Genibrel
Steve Smith Autosports

Martin Motorsports Publications

Competitive Karting $14.95 Plus S&H

A comprehensive guide for the individual who is seriously considering entering the karting field. Complete information on, how to begin, what to buy, and how to prepare a kart for racing. Everything you need to know to be competitive in your very first race. This book offers detailed information never before available to the beginning karter. Here's your chance to gain the competitive edge! You don't have to be a spectator anymore. Karting can put you in the drivers seat where you can experience the thrill of victory first hand. Order your copy today. Only $14.95 plus $2.00 Shipping and handling.

Go-Kart Racing - Chassis Setup $14.95 Plus S&H

Tired of running at the back of the pack. This book will show you how to reduce your lap times without spending hundreds of dollars. CHASSIS SETUP covers the principles involved in good handling as it relates to any kart. Learn what the leaders know. It's not black magic, anyone can do it. The important thing in kart racing is to find out what it takes to make your kart as fast as possible. If you've been buying $600.00 motors and are not going any faster you just may be looking in the wrong place. You can go faster and have more fun doing it. Order today only $14.95 plus $2.00 shipping and handling.

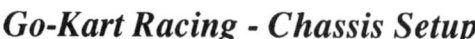

4-Cycle Kart Engines $14.95 Plus S&H

A guide to all 4-cycle engines used in karting today. Also includes chapters on camshafts and computers in karting. A very good book for the rookie karter who really wants basic stock information. This book can get you started on the right foot in the engine department. Order today only $14.95 plus $2.00 shipping and handling.

Karting Tools & Tips $14.95 Plus S&H

Now a book that can save you time and money. Over 125 karting related tools and ideas you can use every day. You don't have to buy a lot of expensive tools to be a competitive karter. You won't beleive the number of labor saving devices lying right under your nose. Karting can be fun and enjoyable. Let Martin Motorsports help you find the way. Order this fine book today. You'll be glad you did. Only $14.95 plus $2.00 shipping and handling.

All books are 8 1/2 x 11, soft cover. These are well prepared, well written books, not copy machine copies. You can be proud to add them to your karting library.

MARTIN MOTORSPORTS

P. O. BOX 12654   FT WAYNE, IND. 46864